William Kay is a former City Editor of *The Times*. He has been in financial journalism for some twenty years, during which time he has followed closely the careers of the businessmen profiled in *Tycoons*. He has also worked on *The London Standard*, *Daily Telegraph* and *The Sunday Times*.

William Kay is the author of *A–Z Guide to Money*, published in 1983.

William Kay

Tycoons

Where they came from and
how they made it

Pan Books London and Sydney

First published 1985 by Judy Piatkus (Publishers) Limited.
This edition published 1986 by Pan Books Ltd,
Cavaye Place, London SW10 9PG
9 8 7 6 5 4 3 2 1
© William Kay 1985
ISBN 0 330 29514 4
Printed and bound in Great Britain by
Cox & Wyman Ltd, Reading

Contents

Acknowledgement

My heartfelt thanks go to the thirteen businessmen who generously agreed to be interviewed for this book. In doing so, they not only gave up several hours of their time to explain the inner workings of their companies to a degree that must have tried their patience: they subsequently took the trouble to read a draft of the chapter devoted to them, and in most cases were confronted with further supplementary questions. They bore the ordeal with great fortitude, and I am grateful to them all.

I also drew extensively from Sir Nigel Broackes' autobiography, *A Growing Concern*, and I am indebted to Barty Phillips for the source material in her book, *Conran and the Habitat Story*. Both volumes are published by Weidenfeld and Nicolson.

I should like to add that several months of the time spent writing this book have been saved with the help of Applied Computer Techniques plc, who were benevolent enough to lend me an Apricot computer and word-processing program. I do not know how I would have managed without it.

Finally, let me confess that any errors that have survived the long-suffering editing of Gill Cormode of Piatkus Books are mine alone.

Introduction

The self-made British millionaire is a peculiar animal. He has to make his fortune in one of the world's most self-effacing and class-ridden countries, where material success is often frowned upon and profit-making is regarded with deep suspicion. The business world is so dimly understood by most people that there are only two commonplace words in the language to describe its leaders: 'proprietor', a synonym for 'owner', and the prosaic 'businessman', which really tells us nothing at all and helps to preserve the ridiculous mystique which envelops the commercial world. So we have imported 'tycoon' from Japan and 'entrepreneur' from France, which more accurately describe the power which businessmen can wield and the enterprising approach they need to build their empires.

'Tycoon' is a Japanese word for a prince or lord, and it was used to explain to foreigners the importance of the shogun, the warlord – as James Clavell's best-selling novel vividly recalled. Most English businessmen shy away from such comparisons, the more so since a tycoon has come to conjure an image of the crew-cut, cigar-chewing boss of a mighty American corporation, grinding the opposition into the ground in relentless pursuit of profit. Above all, many directors of large British companies prefer to play down the emphasis on the power-wielding side of business life. And referring to someone as a tycoon automatically implies that he has succeeded in building an empire around himself, so admitting to the description is thought to look a bit like bragging.

Some of the men interviewed in this book would not be so bashful. Gerald Ronson and Robert Maxwell have the bold, swash-buckling style of the tycoon, and they do not try to hide the fact that all decisions of any importance in their organisations are made or agreed by them. They would, like the shogun, insist that they have developed enduring structures which will long survive their deaths. But they would also accept that in neither case will their dynasties be quite the same without them.

Others would instead fall gratefully on the more modest title of entrepreneur. It has an attractive air of sophistication and subtlety that many businessmen feel they do not get enough credit for in this country. An entrepreneur is literally a 'taker-between', a middle man, which hints at the co-ordinating part of running a business.

But, as the succeeding chapters try to show, there is more to it than that. What these people have done is to conceive an idea and put it into practice by assembling the necessary buildings, machinery and employees. They have then added to and refined the original concept as circumstances changed and as they learned from experience. Above all, they own or control their businesses, which gives them the power and responsibility of taking action.

Perhaps the British like to think that they are too self-effacing for such positive and virile activity. Certainly, it is all of a piece with the British suspicion of anyone who claims to enjoy making profits. To many people, profits can be produced only if someone has been exploited somewhere along the line. The idea of a profit as a reward for providing a service or adding value to a product is alien to such thinking.

Against that cold and at times hostile domestic background, those who become successful at running businesses in this country have to have an almost freakish blend of qualities. For some, like Robert Maxwell or Mark Weinberg, the most valuable quality of all is that they were not born within these shores and so did not suffer from the natives' natural inhibitions. One antidote to that, as John Gunn discovered, was to live abroad for a few formative years. In his case they were spent in Berlin soon after the Wall was erected, a powerful impression with which to return to Britain and reassess our ways. He says that his company, in the fast-moving world of broking money and securities, would not have grown internationally in the way it has without that experience.

There are advantages to being an outsider when someone is starting out in business. You have to be a loner, stick to your guns, be determined to see things through to your goal. Although now-adays help is available in a formal sense, the tyro entrepreneur has few allies, because he has very little to offer in return.

The interviews in this book show that, in the midst of very different family backgrounds and circumstances, all of them have sat back at a certain stage and decided on a clear course of action. Some of that has been discerned with the advantage of hindsight, but there has been a point where the principal theme of their present-day business has crystallised in their mind, and they have pursued that model ever since.

Beyond that, it is difficult to generalise: some left school early, others are graduates; there is a preponderance of only children, and there is one orphan, but several have emerged from large and happy families; some of their fathers had been in business, but with no great success. A few showed signs of their money-making talents in their childhood or early youth, and in some cases that planted the idea of running their own business. But, with the exception of Gerald Ronson, none appears to have had much active encouragement from his parents.

The interviews try to give a reasonable cross-section of tycoons in different stages of development, across a fair spectrum of activities. However, readers will notice that there are two notable omissions in the profile represented in the following pages: women and non-whites. The present book has tried to examine the intrinsic problems and challenges of starting and running a business. Women and the coloured population are beginning to break through in the commercial world, but the stories of how they are doing so are stories of overcoming obstacles of a quite different order and each deserves a book of its own.

The solutions they have had to find have required quite different approaches to the question of building a business. Women have attempted to achieve that with minimal damage to their family life, something which has not been so much of a concern to a significant proportion of the men in this book. But acquiring and maintaining credibility has been the biggest problem for both blacks and women. Bluntly, they have faced an unspoken resistance which it has taken extraordinary persistence and ingenuity to overcome, and only now are there encouraging signs that they are beginning to be treated on an equal footing with their white, male counterparts. Jennifer d'Abo of Ryman and Anita Roddick of The Body Shop, for example, are blazing a trail. The Indian business community is also beginning to emerge at a public level.

The ability to see with a fresh pair of eyes is essential for starting and running a business. You have to spot something that no one else is doing, or that you can do better, for which you think there is going to be a demand at a price which makes it worth your while. Anyone who is content to take life as it comes and accept whatever is offered in the way of a job and a wage should keep doing just that. Peace and contentment are admirable goals but they do not get you very far in the commercial world.

There appear to be plenty of people nursing ideas for their own business who never get round to putting them into practice. They are baffled by the legal requirements and frightened at the thought of having to put up a life's savings before a penny comes back into their embryonic enterprise. But in fact the opportunities for starting your own business today are greater than ever.

The small businessman has been one of the folk heroes of the Thatcher government. Exemplifying the benefits of self-help and independence, he has been a means of diverting attention from the miserable problems of large-scale unemployment. Indeed, the small business has been hailed as an engine for creating jobs and as a constructive way for some of the unemployed simultaneously to invest their redundancy payments and find themselves a new occupation of their own choosing.

To that end, every plan for encouraging new firms has been energetically pursued. Both the Department of Trade and Industry and the Manpower Services Commission offer advice and run courses. Sir Geoffrey Howe introduced the Business Expansion Scheme to give investors tax relief if they put money into young companies. There are dozens of private concerns offering venture capital, from the high street banks to regional enterprise boards.

And yet the dole queues have stubbornly stayed as long as ever. Very few have turned their handshakes, golden or otherwise, into the starting capital for their own business. Millions of pounds of help goes a-begging each year because people do not come forward to claim it. One reason for writing this book is to show how some of the most successful tycoons of the past twenty years got started, in the hope that more will be encouraged to try their hand. As Sir Clive Sinclair said: 'What holds people back from starting businesses is that they think it's very difficult. But it's not at all difficult. That is why I think the more people start their own businesses the better. It might well start a trend, and people won't think it's so magical.'

All the millionaires interviewed for this book began modestly. Sinclair worked from the back room of his flat until the landlord objected. Sir Terence Conran rented a small, rundown workshop in Bethnal Green. Some, like James Gulliver, had enough of a record in business to attract financial backing. Only one admitted to taking out a second mortgage on his house. That was Michael Golder of Kennedy Brookes, and the money went into a restaurant which could have been resold if the worst had come to the worst.

The overriding theme is of people who expanded cautiously, one step at a time, developing the business gradually in the early years until they became confident in themselves and others became confident in their ability to deliver. Indeed, with the possible exception of Gulliver, none considered himself a risk taker and several positively disputed that description. All agreed that they never have and never would commit their companies to any new project which could possibly endanger the whole. However, as Sir Clive Sinclair's cash flow problems in 1985 showed, the price of continued independence is eternal vigilance.

Although in each case the business scene has radically changed since they launched out on their own, their early stories are those of thousands of other fledgling companies. They had an idea or saw an opportunity which they were convinced could be made to earn them a living, and they stuck at it. None of their original schemes could be patented or copyrighted, and the gaps they spotted have long since been closed by imitators and the sheer weight of competition. The only monopolies they have created have been the monopolies on their own reputations.

In that sense, these men are different from the brilliant managers like Sir John Harvey-Jones at ICI or Ernest Saunders at Guinness the brewer, who are employed to take charge of a longstanding established company and develop it. That contribution, although immensely valuable, is of a different order from that of the people who actually start a business from scratch.

However much the creators of enterprises try to minimise the risk, the leap into the unknown demands a degree of courage that is quite different from the decision to join an existing operation, at whatever level. The difference lies in the goodwill that an established business has, the willingness of others to supply it and buy from it, the confidence that its methods work, even if they might need improving. None of these intangible assets is present on day one. They have to be coaxed into life by the energy and persistence of their owners.

The starting point does not require a flash of genius. Even Sinclair, who has become world-famous for his inventiveness, began by selling substandard electronic parts to hobbyists. He had simply noticed that the needs of a hobbyist are not as demanding as those of a company assembling, say, radios or televisions for the general public. So he bought the parts cheaply, for they were being thrown away by the makers, and took big advertisements in the technical press specifying what the various items could and could not do. Readers assumed that if he could afford half-page ads then he must be all right, so they sent in the money. Sinclair has used mail order ever since.

What characterises the entrepreneur is the itch for independence. Any excuse will do. Golder was bored with his academic life and realised that running his own business was the only way for him to build up capital, so he just chose a business he already knew a little about. Stephen Marks felt he was getting a raw deal from the clothing firm he was working for, but did not know what to do about it. Luckily, he had a good friend who appreciated his talents and lent him the money to go it alone. Gulliver and David Thompson chafed when their companies were taken over. They realised that they had to be their own bosses.

But a workable idea and a determined glint in the eye are not enough. The bankruptcy courts are littered with cases testifying to that. The extra ingredient is a survival instinct, to keep a weather eye out for potential disasters or to make sure that the safety nets are in place. Beyond that, what gets a business going is an awareness of where the next take-off point is, and what will be needed to reach it.

Companies do not grow in a straight line. Barring disasters, they tend to climb a series of plateaux. At each level the business is running at a fairly constant size, with a given amount of capital, number of factories and workers, and a fairly fixed management structure. Mind you, it never seems like that to the people who are directly involved. A new company seems to the owners and employees to be in a restless, ever-changing state of barely organised turmoil.

But outsiders tend to see a company in terms of a snapshot. Their opinion of that snapshot decides how much they will lend, supply to or buy from that company. It also colours the way that the trade or national press write about the business. Unfair though it may be, until that outside snapshot changes in the minds of the people dealing with it, the company cannot move on to the next plateau. Sir Nigel Broackes pointed out that what really mattered when he was making his way in the London property market of the 1950s was the fact that the banks and the Sutton Estate, one of the biggest landlords in Mayfair, gave him their backing. 'The credit and faith of such people were what mattered when I was 21, much more than any capital I had or didn't have.'

Golder was acutely conscious of this 'take-off' effect. He had had some experience of the City, and went out of his way to get the shares of his Kennedy Brookes company traded privately by stockbrokers several years before it actually went public. To him, the crucial deal was the takeover of the Mario and Franco chain of Italian trattorias. Before that, he found it hard to convince anyone that his firm could handle an operation of that scale. After it, people came to him with deals.

Of course, it would be wrong to say that the image is all that matters. That is a common enough trap. The penalties of overblowing the snapshot to the outside world are that people cease to believe the picture that is presented to them, and begin to adjust the focus for themselves. But the need to be known is vital. All those interviewed spoke with varying degrees of bitterness about being in the shadows and misunderstood. Sir Terence Conran, in particular, remembers being refused money to pay the week's wages because a vital cheque had not been cleared. Harry Goodman had to scour the world before he could find a bank to lend the money for Air Europe's first plane – and then it was a Japanese lender who demanded six per cent over the inter-bank rate.

Happily, the British banks have changed their outlook for the better since those days. The threatened wave of company failures towards the end of the 1970s made them rethink their attitude towards their business clients. If they had applied the old rules, there would have been a domino effect of frightening proportions. The result was a far more tolerant and creative approach to the problems of the corporate sector.

That has given rise to the blossoming of the management buy-out, where the management of a company or one of its subsidiaries buys control of it with the help of a hefty loan. This is a variation on the principle which enabled Gulliver to launch out on his own when he left Fine Fare. He had shown his paces there, and a group of institutions took over Oriel Foods for him to run. To show he was serious about it, he had to borrow £1 million to buy 29 per cent of the shares for himself. Interest of more than £100,000 a year was ticking up on that loan, and he was not entirely unhappy to see Oriel taken over a couple of years later in a cash deal which made him a millionaire. When he set up on his own again, he had little trouble finding the backing to build Argyll Group, one of the biggest supermarket groups in the country.

Gulliver took as one of his golden rules the principle that it is better to buy businesses during a recession, when they can be had cheaply. He admitted that it was by no means an original idea. He got it from Paul Getty, but it is a recurrent theme of the histories in this book. David Thompson has turned his Hillsdown Holdings into one of Britain's major food manufacturers by buying firms like Lockwoods and Smedley's from the receiver. Maxwell rescued British Printing Corporation from the brink of collapse and cut costs there by £600,000 a week. It is a basic but often forgotten fact of business life that if the costs are low enough, it is harder to go bust and there is room to breathe and expand.

Keeping the costs down also helps to keep the business simple. The tycoon can afford a finance department and all the computerised systems that money can buy. But when they began, all each of them had was the computer inside his head. As their businesses grew, they had to keep hold of certain key numbers. In that way, even if they could no longer know exactly what was going on in every cranny of their operations, at least they had a signalling system to tell them if something was amiss.

There is nothing startlingly clever about the numbers that matter: cash flow, money in the bank, profit margins, orders, costs, debtors, creditors. Every successful entrepreneur has two or three favourites out of this list, which he follows on a daily basis. One of the most complicated businesses is life insurance, but even there Weinberg was able to reduce it to a matter of the profits on the policies and the expenses of running the business. The hard work lies in getting the premiums right for the sort of policy he wants to sell. In the same way, Goodman reckons he can work out the value of Intasun within seconds, largely by checking the current state of the holiday bookings. If the brochure has been priced correctly, the rest falls into place.

Broackes has delegated most of the number-crunching to his chief executive, Eric Parker, but they operate by imposing self-discipline on the people who run the individual subsidiaries: they are charged or credited with interest, according to whether their bank balance is in the red or not. That makes the divisional chiefs run fast to stay in the black or come up with a good reason why not. The carrot and the stick are among the oldest management tools, but the evidence is that they are as popular as they ever were.

Where there is a group of fairly autonomous divisions, the usual practice is to make the head of each make their own forecasts for the following year, on a month-by-month basis. Then, as each month goes by, the head office team pulls them in to explain the difference between the prediction and the actual outcome. 'We soon get to know the optimists and the pessimists,' said Thompson. Much depends at this stage on the strength of the questioning and the refusal of the man at the top to accept excuses. Thompson prefers to have last month's excuses set down in writing so that the hapless executive cannot wriggle out of them the next time. 'Then it will be easier for him to admit he has been doing something the wrong way, if that's the problem,' he pointed out.

That can be the hardest thing to do in any walk of life. Despite their supposed ruthlessness, the modern British tycoon does not find it easy to get rid of employees who do not come up to scratch. Maxwell is perhaps more matter-of-fact about dropping people who do not fit in, but they all see it as a failure on their own part if one of their executives has to go. Even allowing for a generous ration of crocodile tears and a wish to appear warm-hearted in public, several admitted that they put off the decision for far too long in some cases, out of a reluctance to tell someone he was finished.

'The longer you leave it the more painful it is for both sides,' admitted Weinberg. 'It happens eventually, when it blows up in your face. It's much more agonising then.' They would far rather move a person sideways. 'You can always play around with titles, to make it easier for the man to accept,' said Goodman. One or two rely on promoting people within the group whom they have known for some years, so that they have a better idea of their capabilities. As most of these companies have had good growth records, they have not often had to cope with large-scale redundancies among the workforce. This has normally happened after a takeover, and then the blame has been firmly placed with the former owners.

However, most of our tycoons have suffered their own crises from time to time. Although it is now a fading memory, the secondary banking collapse of 1974 took a severe toll, as Thompson admitted. Maxwell was in the wilderness for several years after the Leasco affair. And 1985 will not go down as a good year for Sir Clive Sinclair. The launch of the C5 electric car misfired, and overstocking by retailers led to an alarming drop in orders for home computers during the first half of the year, with the inevitable consequences for Sinclair's cash flow and subsequent rescue bids.

During the writing of this book, two of the subjects apart from Sinclair have chosen to be taken over. Weinberg, who built Hambro Life up from a value of £1 million to £200 million in little more than a decade, accepted a bid from BAT Industries, the giant tobacco group which already owned Eagle Star Insurance. He agreed to stay with the group for five years after the deal, and has also been helping to set up a new system of regulations for the savings and securities industry.

Noel Lister, on the other hand, has sold out completely from his MFI Furniture Industries and is sailing over the horizon in a 103-foot racing yacht. He is one of the few to take the money and go, raising the question of what budding tycoons go into business for, and what makes them keep at it long after they had made more money than they can spend in several lifetimes.

A large proportion, particularly those like Marks of French Connection, who have floated their companies on the Stock Exchange's Unlisted Securities Market, have no choice because they could not sell their shares – barring a takeover. Marks owned 82 per cent of French Connection when he went public, so if he tried to sell more than a small slice of that the price would collapse against him. After all, French Connection without Marks would hardly be the same thing.

But that is not the whole story. Age is an important factor. Most entrepreneurs could not just retire if they sold their businesses. They are too young to do nothing. Maxwell is the only one of the present selection over sixty. So they would have to find something else to occupy them, and why start from scratch all over again?

Becoming a millionaire is only a minor milestone on the way to far grander objectives. That has lost its attraction now that, thanks to inflation, there are so many of them. By the time they realise that they never need to work again, they are so far past that barrier that they are already looking ahead to the next goal.

In some cases they have a vision. Conran has a vision of the way he would like us to be dressed, and how our homes should look. More commonly, tycoons have a vision of what they would like the company to be within a foreseeable span of five or ten years. Either it should be dominant in its own industry, or should be hitting a certain size in money terms, or climbing up the league table of the biggest companies in the country. Ronson conceded that his still privately owned Heron International would never be the biggest, 'because you've got firms like BP and Shell up there,' but he believed that a place in the top ten was a realistic aim. Meanwhile, he was intent on catching Littlewoods as Britain's biggest private company.

These are all routes to respectability and status. Tycoons cherish above all the respect of their equals, the only other people whom they feel truly understand them. The knighthoods and occasional peerages that go with success only help to confirm their status in their own eyes. But on a day-to-day level, the constantly shifting strategies and tactics of the business world are a continual source of fascination for those in a position to decide on the moves. The rules of the game impose restraints, of course. But they are far more acceptable restraints than the one the rest of the population has to live with: that of having to be subject to the whims and personal tastes of an employer.

Sir Nigel Broackes

Sir Nigel Broackes is the effortless opportunist. On his own account, he went into property when the chances of success were better than they had been for a generation, and he went on to make his fortune by expanding into construction, hotels, shipping and publishing at a time when each of those industries was in or near the doldrums. But he is also a throwback to an earlier age: Sir Nigel paints a convincing picture of a nineteenth-century liberal determined to make his own way as a means of achieving personal freedom.

'I never had any desire to be my own boss, in terms of owning my own company,' he explained. 'I was determined to do something that gave me more scope and freedom. I did not want to be pinned down. As soon as I got the property idea together and saw how it was going to generate capital, my wish was to lead that business rather than just build up equity and a bank balance. What I wanted was to be managing director or chairman of a large unit, which is where I felt most comfortable.'

By the age of 34 he had done just that. In the process he had created Trafalgar House, and turned it into a substantial property and construction group, including Trollope & Colls and Ideal Homes. Since then he has expanded it into one of the forty biggest companies in Britain, owning the London Ritz Hotel, the QE2 and the rest of the Cunard shipping line, the Scott Lithgow shipyard and extensive interests in North Sea oil. It has been a remarkable personal triumph, accomplished with an apparent ease which belies an unwavering determination.

Broackes emerged as a stock market force in the early 1960s, a year or two before financial whizz-kids like Jim Slater and Oliver Jessel were beginning to dazzle the City. He was soon bracketed with them in the public mind, but Trafalgar went on from strength to strength while Slater and Jessel's companies of that era fell by the wayside. As Sir Nigel's business has become more substantial and broadly-based, so has he. He has filled out, and his taste for fine wine and good cigars has given his voice a plummy resonance that is more often found in fictional men of property than a real one.

The grandson of a civil engineer and son of a Yorkshire solicitor, Broackes left his public school, Stowe, at the age of sixteen in a mood of disenchantment. He had had a rebellious childhood, and was flogged by his prep school headmaster for playing with an incendiary bomb which went off. When he was twelve he made radio receivers and sold them for a 100 per cent profit. At Stowe he defied school rules by keeping a 500 cc motor bike and selling gin under the counter at school parties.

Unhappy and discontented, the young Broackes deferred National Service and went straight into the City, to work for a Lloyd's insurance underwriting agency where the father of a school friend was one of the directors. But he found the under-writers' boxes, as their desks on the trading floor are known, too claustrophobic.

Instead, Broackes found himself walking around the building sites which were springing up in the City in the years after the Second World War, and marvelled at the shining new office blocks which were being constructed. In his autobiography, *A Growing Concern*, Sir Nigel wrote: 'At that time I had no concept of the role of the entrepreneur and the developer, and I just wanted to become the effective cause that made such things happen. I would happily have taken a job with no prospects beyond a salary and a pension to be able to do so.'

By the time he emerged from National Service with the Hussars, Broackes still cherished his dream of putting up large buildings, but was rapidly dropping the idea of settling for a salary and a pension. He was due to come into a legacy of £30,000 when he was 21, enough in those days to become a member of Lloyd's. That, together with his salary, would have given him an income of about £10,000 a year by the late 1950s – a handsome sum in those days, worth at least £50,000 today, in return for not too much work.

It says a lot about Broackes' view of the world then, that he was so willing to toss away a prospect which most people would have taken with both hands. He had no definite plans, and within a year or so of collecting the legacy it had all gone down the drain in early business ventures. He was already married and had a child. Sir Nigel recalled: 'What was important at the start of my career was not the legacy I received, but losing that legacy. That meant I had to do something to stay afloat.'

The commercial world of London in the 1950s was a shifting mass of deals and contacts and new ventures taking advantage of the new techniques and opportunities presented by the aftermath of war. Noel Lister, one of the founders of the MFI Furniture Group, was feeling his way through the north London part of this cloudy undergrowth by dealing in war surplus goods. Broackes found himself, through a series of chance acquaintances, simultaneously in two very different territories. The sleazy, half-glamorous south London second-hand car trade of that time nearly bankrupted him. On the other side of the Thames, meanwhile, he was making the contacts which would put him on the road to a fortune.

· This was a time when Broackes was building contacts very rapidly. Some stood him in good stead for the future: others brought him to the brink of bankruptcy. He met a second-hand car dealer called Peter Buckley in the King's Road and went into business with him. Buckley became insolvent and Broackes lost his profits from the venture, but managed to take out his original stake. However, through Buckley, Broackes met Michael Rawlence, who was to introduce him to the West End property world. On holiday in Jersey he met Shane Milward, a property developer who later gave Broackes his first major property development job. At a party in Kensington he met a solicitor, John Batt, who became a lifelong friend but more immediately led Broackes into the small-time suburban business environment.

Broackes was spending hours poring over legal statutes, company accounts and manuals on commercial practice. He recalled: 'My objective, quite simply, was to know more about law than people who were not lawyers, more about accounts than people who were not accountants, and so on, across the field of business, with some extra emphasis on the numerous professions that relate in some way to property.'

Broackes took to visiting Batt's office and having lunch with him at the Dog and Fox near Wimbledon underground station. Through his brief experience in the car trade Broackes had decided to set up a hire purchase firm, but he also wanted to invest in some other businesses for the experience. And experience is precisely what he got.

One of his early investments was in Tratt Plastics, making cheap injection-moulded toys. It was small enough for Broackes to buy forty per cent of the shares and claim a seat on the board. Tratt expanded quickly to turning out components for Ford cars and trinkets for chewing gum machines. But it was all too good to be true. The reason they were getting so much business was that they were simply not charging enough. By the time this came to light the firm could not meet its bills for raw materials. Tratt went into liquidation.

At just about the same time the hire purchase venture was also going sour. Using money from friends and stockbroking contacts, Broackes lent on to the car trade through a company called Southern Counties Discount. He was borrowing at seven per cent and charging more than twenty per cent. It sounded cast iron – until Broackes went outside cars to lend to a tallyman selling clothes door-to-door and collecting weekly repayments. The tally-man in question took to forging six copies of every credit agreement and collecting cash from six different hire purchase companies. He was found guilty of fraud and Broackes lost nearly all his money.

But Broackes said: 'The only way to go was forward, and other, better projects were already in hand.' His interest in buildings led him into converting terraced houses in the smarter areas of London into individual flats. His first project was a pair of workmen's cottages in Markham Street, Chelsea. He paid £7,600 for them, spent as much again on converting them and just about managed to get his money back.

Meanwhile, the more prosperous end of his spectrum of connections were coming good. The stockbroker, David Fremantle, was chairman of a small investment trust and started a property company which Broackes did some work for. The firm laboured under the name of Eastern International Property Investments, but this was the cradle of what was eventually to be renamed Trafalgar House, after a property they acquired near Trafalgar Square in Whitehall.

The estate agent, Shane Milward, offered Broackes a development scheme in Piccadilly for which Milward did not have the money to handle himself. The property, a block of rundown flats called Green Park House, was the making of Broackes' career. Like Milward, he did not have the money to modernise the flats himself, but he passed it on to Eastern in return for being allowed to do the work.

That job took Broackes into the West End property business in 1956, at the age of 22, and brought him into contact with the Sutton Estate, which owned large tracts of Mayfair and Soho, and was therefore a powerful patron of property developers. Sir Nigel pointed out: 'It is hard to get into central London development work if one has not already a proven record of previous competence and success. I was determined to impress the Sutton Estate so as to be considered for some of their commercial schemes. They are fastidious in their relationships with developers and highly selective with regard to whom they allow to operate on the estate. Thus Green Park House was directly to lead to office building opportunities where the figures were very much larger – first ten times, then 100 times, and so on.'

And after Broackes' experience in Markham Street, he decided not to take any chances with the quality of the building work. He called in the best builders he could find, Trollope & Colls, where unbeknown to him Victor Matthews was working as a contracts manager; later Matthews became managing director of Trafalgar House and Broackes' right-hand man.

Broackes' next stroke was to get himself set up in a West End office. At this stage he had been based in Brompton Road, down by Harrods, but he felt that even there he was out of the mainstream of the property business. Luckily, Fremantle wanted to diversify Eastern into a service industry, and the most closely related service to property is estate agency. Broackes introduced Collins & Collins and Rawlence & Squarey as the agents to sell the leases on the newly modernised flats in Green Park House, where it turned out that the owner of half the shares wanted to retire. Eastern bought that stake and installed Broackes in the Chesterfield Gardens office, which he proceeded to use as his launch pad and learn the nuts and bolts of estate agency at the same time.

'This was really quite a short period of history following the abolition of building licences in 1952. All the activity of many years was compressed into a short period. There weren't many people who remembered how to do it: there were only people who had been in property since the great depression, and there was no one who had over four years' experience more than I had.

'The Sutton Estate and the banks were very important, and the credit and faith of such people were what mattered when I was 21, much more than any capital I had or didn't have. It would be just as true today, but the opportunities are so much more restricted, and the financial background to property has changed so radically. In those days property was a means to create an asset from a very small residual equity. Some schemes were worth fifty per cent more than cost. Interest rates were lower than the running yield. So one created an equity out of thin air.'

Although interest rates are a lot higher today, the recent revival in the London property market has shown that it is still possible to put together the sort of deals that Broackes pulled off in those early days. Property is as much as anything else an ideas business, and the opportunities are always there for anyone who can visualise winning schemes and persuade the powers that be to let them go ahead.

For Broackes, the deals began to pile up in the two years after he established himself in Chesterfield Gardens, and so did his own personal wealth. He reached the point where he had to decide whether to make it on his own as a developer or take a stake in Eastern. Matters came to a head when he bought the lease of a bomb site in Great Cumberland Place, just off Marble Arch, and set about building a small block of six flats and a maisonette there. Fremantle realised that if he did not do something soon Broackes would have gradually broken away, and Eastern was in any case becoming financially stretched. So he sold Broackes 15,000 newly created shares for £1 each, equal to 41.66 per cent of the enlarged company, and Broackes became managing director.

The late Lord Crowther, former editor of *The Economist*, was a friend of one of the other Eastern directors, and was invited on the board to lend weight to what was still a fairly modest property company. He was also on the board of Commercial Union Assurance Company, and proved a vital link in CU becoming Trafalgar's main backer and source of funds. CU boosted Eastern by selling it a property company, the one which had a lease on Trafalgar House and led to the change in the group's name. A new building firm began to win tenders for Trafalgar contracts: it was Bridge Walker, owned by Victor Matthews, and that is how Broackes and Matthews first met.

By 1963 Trafalgar House had grown sufficiently to go public, putting a value of £330,000 on the 28-year-old Broackes' personal shareholding. He and his wife, Joyce, had two children then, and they were living in a large house in Holland Park, London. Soon afterwards Broackes bought his first Rolls-Royce. 'I reached the point of financial independence about then,' Sir Nigel recalled, 'but I am not dominated by the idea of financial independence.' Instead, he became dominated by a restless urge to take Trafalgar in new directions.

'Property takes a lot of patience,' said Sir Nigel, 'and the Achilles heel of the property developer is boredom or the fact that he is insecurely financed. I needed something more creative, so we went into housebuilding. As we got more flats – we had about 1,600 – we were spending £250,000 a month repairing twenty years of bad management and forty or fifty years of rent control. The amount we were spending on construction meant we had to have a financial interest in a builder. It was a question of having control, because we were in a position where we were saying, "Do it in eight to ten weeks and let us know what it costs". That was ridiculous.'

The relationship between Broackes and Matthews grew so close that Broackes effectively stopped another company from taking over Bridge Walker, Matthews' construction firm. Instead, Trafalgar bought control of Bridge Walker in 1964. At about this time another change started to appear over the horizon, one which was to make Broackes all the more determined to lessen his dependence on property, pure and simple.

It was becoming increasingly likely that the Labour party was going to win the forthcoming general election. Under Harold Wilson, they had signalled their intention to introduce a form of Corporation Tax on companies instead of the straightforward Profits Tax. The effect of this would be to tax twice over any profits that were handed over to shareholders as dividends. Profits that were reinvested in the business would be taxed only once.

The aim of the change was precisely that: to encourage companies to invest. But the traditional purpose of property companies had been to generate a flow of rental income which could be passed on to shareholders in dividends. Broackes flew to the US and Australia to see for himself how their property industries had adapted to Corporation Tax. He found that the traditional British type of company simply did not exist.

In the new climate it would be self-defeating to take all the rents and money from selling properties and reinvest it in new properties, as the lack of dividends would depress their share prices and make them vulnerable to being taken over. Instead, Broackes argued, it made far more sense to use the money positively by investing in trading activities relating to property.

'The changes in the tax position when Corporation Tax was introduced were compatible with my inclinations,' said Sir Nigel. 'My choice was right for me: I saw the implications earlier than anyone else because I wanted to.' He drew up a list of the ten public companies most likely to be hit by the new tax. On that list was Trollope & Colls, but before he could make a move for it he was asked if Trafalgar would like to take over Ideal Building Corporation, a leading housebuilder. That done, Trafalgar then went for Trollope in the teeth of opposition from the board of the construction company and a rival offer from the Church Commissioners. Broackes won with a bid worth £14 million.

From that base, expansion was rapid over the next ten years. Construction led to civil engineering, which led to hotels and shipping. In 1971 Trafalgar took over Cunard, which then had the QE2 and two other passenger ships, 67 cargo ships and the Lunn Poly and Sunair package tour businesses.

Sir Nigel explained: 'When we studied it, Cunard had these tax advantages, which were in the books, and so already built into the price of the company. What we believed was that the tax advantages were groupable, so that they could be offset against Trafalgar's other profits. That had not been done like that before. Cunard was also attractive in its own right, but no one will believe that we did not do it purely for the tax advantages. Cunard cost us £27 million, and it has earned profits in the region of about £20 million a year and saved us tax of about £100 million in all.'

The Cunard deal established Trafalgar as one of the first of the new breed of industrial groupings, buying undervalued assets to develop them rather than strip them. It also linked Sir Nigel in the stock market's eyes with a taste for the grand old names of British business. In 1971 he tried to buy both Thomas Cook, the travel firm, and Rolls-Royce Motors, two early privatisations. And even before Trafalgar acquired Cunard, the company had begun to build a stake in the Savoy Hotel Group, which apart from the Savoy included Claridge's, the Connaught and the Berkeley within a few miles of one another in the West End.

The Savoy Group was a prize sought by every hotelier in London, but was and is extremely hard to get at. The reason lies in the shape of the company's share capital, which puts the bulk of the voting power in the hands of a relatively small number of 'B' shares. These are tightly held by the Savoy's directors and in trusts where those same directors are the trustees. This system was voted into existence by the shareholders back in the 1950s precisely to thwart the threat of a takeover. Since then the Stock Exchange has encouraged companies to follow the principle of 'one share, one vote', and most have come into line. Not the Savoy, though.

Sir Nigel knew that the odds were stacked against him when he started buying Savoy shares. The only ones that were easily available on the stock market were the low-voting 'A' shares, but like other would-be bidders Sir Nigel reckoned that there might be a change in the law and the door to control of the Savoy might be unlocked. After ten years he gave up knocking on the door and sold the shares to the late Sir Maxwell Joseph of Grand Metropolitan. The latest supplicant is Trusthouse Forte, but the Savoy's door seems as firmly bolted as ever.

By the time he had passed that parcel to Sir Maxwell, Sir Nigel had partly satisfied his appetite for a grand London hotel.

Trafalgar had bought the Ritz. There, the management was growing old, and had neither the energy nor the inclination to cling to
control. Trafalgar put a casino in the basement, shops on the
ground floor and spent £5 million restoring and extending the
building. The dining room is once again one of the most elegant in
London, especially on a sunny day.

During the 1970s Sir Nigel became less involved with the day-
to-day management of Trafalgar. He had not personally handled a
property development for the group since 1966, when he built
Broadwalk House, a block of flats at Hyde Park Gate. Trafalgar
was being run by a triumvirate of Broackes, Matthews and Eric
Parker, a chartered accountant who had been recruited from
Taylor Woodrow in 1966 to be chief accountant for Bridge
Walker.

Parker explained how it works today. 'The executive committee
has power delegated to it by the main board, and the committee has
in turn delegated powers to me as chief executive. I have a series of
divisional heads reporting to me, and I meet them once a week or
once a fortnight with a formal agenda. The divisional heads report
their previous month's performance and their current month's
forecast.' He had just been clearing a £50 million tender for a steel
contract in Saudi Arabia, and the previous day the in-tray contained a sheaf of proposals for buying housing land.

'In general, the initiatives come from the managing directors of
the operating subsidiaries,' he said, 'and they put them to their
divisional managing director. We try to have an effective, fast-
moving divisional control. I monitor profit and cash flows, and
weekly borrowings. Every week we get the worldwide borrowing
figures from each of the 300 subsidiaries. We charge them interest
if they are net borrowers, and credit them if they are in credit. We
take an overall view of the group once a month, making forecasts
for the current financial year to September and the following
financial year, then every third month we look five years ahead.
We don't take that too seriously: you're tending to look at trends,
whether a business is producing or absorbing cash.'

It is vital for a diversified group like Trafalgar to balance out the
ebbs and flows of cash. Housebuilding absorbs it but construction
generates it. Shipping, Parker pointed out, makes very lumpy

demands for money when new vessels have to be bought or a refit carried out. Oil or gas makes sense only if the operator can afford to look ahead ten years or more. 'Otherwise, you might say it was a hopeless business,' he smiled. Clearly, Trafalgar thinks otherwise. Parker and Broackes lunch together every Monday, and meet between-times during the rest of the week – except Fridays. 'Nigel hasn't come in to the office on a Friday for as long as I can remember,' he said.

As early as 1969 Broackes had begun to examine himself and his motivation. He records in his book that he was 'fearful of binding myself more inextricably to what I had done much to create', and that this might lead to a lifetime on what was even then beginning to feel like a treadmill. He diagnoses this mood as a premature attack of mid-life crisis, for he was only 35 when it began to take hold. But the effects were twofold. He drew back to take a more strategic view of the business, and began to divert his attention elsewhere.

He was recognised as one of the brightest of his generation of entrepreneurs, and the government led by Edward Heath from 1970 to 1974 tried to draw on the talents of Broackes and some of his contemporaries. He had got to know Sir Keith Joseph through charitable housing work in the 1960s, and Michael Heseltine through his role in housing and office development permits in 1970. On one bizarre occasion Heath invited him to a dinner at Chequers with Jim Slater, Lord Rothschild and assorted ministers. This was followed by one or two government appointments, culminating in the chairmanship of the London Docklands Development Corporation under the Thatcher government of 1979.

Trafalgar was running itself perfectly well during this time, to the point where it was piling up cash, but it inevitably showed signs of lacking the drive from the top as Broackes became involved elsewhere. Matthews, too, was in something of a rut. By 1977 he was even beginning to talk of retirement, and Broackes was searching for a new challenge to throw at his old partner. For the previous two years they had been interested in Beaverbrook Newspapers, the Daily and Sunday Express group which had been founded by Lord Beaverbrook before the First World War.

Like the Ritz and Cunard, it owned a famous name but had fallen on difficult times.

In recent years there has been a ready queue of bidders for any Fleet Street group that comes on the market. The belief is that the printing unions are on the retreat and the introduction of computer-based production systems will make them enormously profitable once again. So when it appeared that Sir Max Aitken, Lord Beaverbrook's son, was prepared to sell the family business there was no shortage of would-be suitors. Associated Newspapers, owner of the *Daily Mail* and Beaverbrook's oldest rival, stood to gain most by merging the Mail and Express titles. Sir James Goldsmith and Tiny Rowland publicly declared their interest. But Trafalgar was hovering in the background, Aitken's preferred choice if a deal could be reached, and although Beaverbrook was a public company it was, like the Savoy, effectively controlled by family trusts. So the situation that had denied Trafalgar the Savoy gave it Beaverbrook, for £14 million.

Sir Nigel explained: 'Beaverbrook was a different situation because it had unused property and modernised plant. They had spent recklessly by the standards of these days. The reason Beaverbrook had been so open-handed was the share structure, the large amount of non-voters, and the fact that this was a political thing for Lord Beaverbrook. Among the unused properties, the old Standard site in Shoe Lane was a good one. We redeveloped it and let it to Coopers and Lybrand, the accountants.'

Express Newspapers, as it was renamed, was never fully integrated into the Trafalgar organisation. It came under Matthews' personal control, and it was he rather than Broackes who became identified with it in the public mind. Matthews became a press baron, and he revelled in it. Broackes was content to take a back seat. They took over Morgan Grampian, the magazine publisher based in Woolwich, for £20 million, and launched a new national newspaper, the *Daily Star*, to mop up some of the Express's unused capacity.

But, according to Sir Nigel, the operation never made the profits he had hoped to see from it. When in 1981 Sir Geoffrey Howe changed the tax rules to make it easier for companies to demerge subsidiaries, the Express group was a natural target. It was floated on to the stock market in its own right as Fleet Holdings. Trafalgar accomplished this as a free issue to its own shareholders, and earlier aspirations were fulfilled as the new Fleet shares gradually rose from around 20p each to 375p, the price at which the company was taken over by United Newspapers in 1985.

In the meantime, Eric Parker had progressed formidably through the group from joining Bridge Walker in 1966 to becoming group managing director of the whole of Trafalgar in 1978. Broackes described his own post-1969 role as 'non executive, but *fairly* full-time', and when he took on the London Docklands chairmanship in 1980 he relinquished other outside appointments ranging from a governorship of his old school, Stowe, to membership of the Council of the Victoria & Albert Museum, trusteeship of the Royal Opera House, Covent Garden, and membership of the board of the Tote!

Docklands was one of the very few interventionist initiatives of the Thatcher government, and perhaps its most successful. For Sir Nigel, it meant a renewed challenge, testing social and political skills as well as property, construction and financial abilities which by then had been established. The result is now indisputably a matter of record and, at the age of fifty, the word '*fairly*' recedes as so many of the team of twenty years ago remain in place. A £15 million family shareholding in Trafalgar demonstrates the personal commitment, and other resources support the objectives listed at the beginning of this chapter.

'I am much busier here than I was in the 1970s,' he said. 'I have exorcised the ghost of feeling trapped.' In 1984 he made an ambitious bid for another grand old trading name, P & O, which still officially goes under the magnificent name of the Peninsular and Oriental Steam Navigation Company. It would have fitted well with Trafalgar, as both were in shipping and construction: P & O owns Bovis. But the bid was referred to the Monopolies and Mergers Commission, and P & O used the breathing space to appoint a new chairman, Sir Jeffrey Sterling, who managed to turn the ailing group round sufficiently to see off Trafalgar.

Nothing daunted, Sir Nigel declared: 'We are transforming Trafalgar. We have got a good board, with a fair proportion of its members in their forties. As to how it will develop, I never make any apologies for being an opportunist. We have not got any radical departure in mind, and there is nothing new that we have to have. The theme of the group today is highly integrated and highly motivated. This is a team. Eric Parker works far harder than I do, and has done for some years. We got a reputation as a financial organisation because the rest of British industry was extremely ill-educated. There were a lot of backwoodsmen around. After the war Britain was in a state of lethargy, which gave us a lot of opportunities. So our financial skills were that much more conspicuous.'

Sir Nigel still has his eye on the monumental project that will set the seal on his place in business history. In 1984 he became chairman of EuroRoute, the ambitious bridge and tunnel project which for a long time was the frontrunner in the race to be allowed to build the historic fixed link across the English Channel. But in the end EuroRoute was beaten to it by the Channel Tunnel Group. Nevertheless, Sir Nigel is unlikely to sit still for long. We can expect him to emerge at the head of further ambitious projects in the next few years.

Sir Terence Conran

Sir Terence Conran is a figure of awe, mystique and fascination to a generation which has furnished its homes to his urbane taste. His immensely successful Habitat chain has changed the face of shopping in Britain. It instantly captured the imagination by putting thoughtfully designed goods in an environment which made existing furniture shops of those days seem stuffy and depressing.

More recently he has taken over Mothercare and Richard Shops, Heals and British Home Stores, to form the Storehouse group. The result is a company turning over more than £1 billion a year through around 870 stores in nine countries from Bermuda to Japan, Singapore to Holland. It employs the equivalent of 22,000 full-time staff.

It would be surprising if that were the end of the story. Now in his fifties, Sir Terence has found a retailing formula which could fit into almost any corner of the high street. By the time he has finished, it probably will. Yet the most remarkable fact about Conran's career is how, in the vital early stages, he was doing little more than reacting to events, trying to overcome problems, before it dawned on him that he had created a substantial business with an independent life of its own.

Born in Esher, Surrey, in 1931, Conran's earliest memory of his latent fascination with interior design was being struck by the beauty of an aunt's house in Devon. He admits that his mother was a profound influence, encouraging his boyhood talent and spurring him on to produce work she would be proud of. He went to Bryanston, the progressive boys' public school, during the 1940s, where he discovered the delights of pottery under a teacher with the storybook name of Don Potter.

A party that got out of hand was enough for Conran to be

expelled in his last term at Bryanston, and he went straight to the Central School of Art and Design, where he specialised in textile design. He was quickly spotted as one of the brightest prospects, and got a job with the Rayon Design Centre in London. The director of that Centre was Dennis Lennon, the architect, who left to set up his own private practice, taking Conran with him.

Their first major project was a series of contributions to the Festival of Britain, which was held on the South Bank in 1951 to celebrate the 100th anniversary of the Great Exhibition in Hyde Park. It was seized on as an opportunity to declare an end to the drabness of the Second World War and its immediate aftermath of ration books and shortages. Some of Conran's first furniture and fabric designs were on show in the Homes and Garden Pavilion.

'We worked hard and even enthusiastically on the Festival of Britain,' said Sir Terence. 'It was supposed to be a great industrial resurgence, and we thought that work would come pouring in after that. But it just dried up. So Dennis Lennon could not afford the £8 a week he was paying me. I was virtually forced to start up on my own.'

He started in the simplest possible way, with a workshop in Bethnal Green. He sold the furniture, and supplemented his income with some freelance textile design work. 'I had no panting ambition to be an entrepreneur, nor did I see my life rolling forward in some grand plan.' But he was becoming well known in London design circles, and put on a display of furniture at Simpson's, the Piccadilly store. This was at a time when he was using the London underground to deliver furniture. But there was enough work about for him to begin employing one or two people.

It was a time of struggle, and Sir Terence is bitter about some of the difficulties he faced then. 'I contrast the enormous amount of advice and training available now with the situation in those days, when everyone seemed to be trying to push you out of business. There was no help, and my bank manager was straightforwardly obstructive. One week he refused to give me the money to pay the wages, even though I had just given him a cheque which would have covered it. He insisted on clearing the cheque, even though he only had to pick up the phone to make sure it was all right.' Even now, nearly thirty years later, Sir Terence's disgust is still apparent. 'At a time when the entrepreneur was supposed to be important to Britain's recovery after the war, it was depressing, but I didn't know any better.'

But eventually he managed to find a bank manager who would take him seriously. And he had inherited the family business name, Conran & Co., along with some useful tax losses. His father had been an importer with warehouses near the London docks. When the Germans bombed those warehouses, he went to work for a customer, leaving the company dormant.

'I was by this time absolutely determined to make a success out of it. I had started to employ people, and I had responsibility for them. I was always just making ends meet.'

Conran's furniture was beginning to find its way into the West End department stores, but it must have been hard to see how the business could be expanded. It was a workshop rather than a factory operation, and the profits were not big enough to enable Conran to make any sizeable investment in extra capacity. But then an opportunity came his way which provided precisely the windfall he needed.

Sir Terence recalled: 'I had a landlord who was short of money. We sat and thought about what to do. At that time there were no restaurants for young people. The espresso coffee machine had just come into Britain, and one or two coffee bars were opening. Otherwise at the cheap end it was either Lyons cafeterias or a pub. There were no cheap restaurants for young people like there are today.'

So they each put £100 into opening a café they called the Soup Kitchen, just off the Strand in London. The only hot food it sold was soup, and coffee made on a Gaggia espresso machine Conran brought back by car from Italy. He had got what little catering experience he had from a spell washing up in a Paris restaurant kitchen. That was where he had noticed how easy it was to make soup. You did not need a trained chef. 'All you need is a huge bunsen burner and a huge stock pot,' Sir Terence explained. 'You could get the bones for practically nothing. We used that and one or two other things to make a base, and we could draw that off into smaller vats to produce the individual flavours.' The menu was topped off with French bread, butter, Cheddar cheese and apple flan. A pint of soup cost the equivalent of 4p.

It quickly caught on as the smart place to be seen in, and another three were opened – including a disastrous one in Cambridge, where the students soon realised that they could linger all night for their 4p. But the London branches flourished, until Conran and his partner fell out. 'We were doing so well that he wanted to introduce hot meals, but I thought that that would complicate the thing.' So the Conran share of the business was bought out for £2,500, a large amount of money in the 1950s.

'That provided me with the first bit of real capital I had ever had,' he said, and he proceeded to spray it round a bewildering range of projects as he became used to spotting opportunities.

One of them was another catering venture, which he called the Orrery, in King's Road. It contained a coffee bar and a restaurant opening out on to a big paved garden at the back. All of a sudden, hot meals did not seem such a bad idea and although he sold the Orrery within a year or so his interest in restaurants remains. The Orrery was important to Conran in another way. It was there he met the future Shirley Conran.

Shirley and Terence married in 1956 and divorced seven years later. They produced Jasper, now one of the hottest properties in the fashion world, and Sebastian, who designs for Conran Associates. Despite remarrying, Shirley retained the Conran name, which has been a bone of some contention, and went on to make a fortune by writing the *Superwoman* advice book and racy novels like *Lace*. In 1963 Terence Conran wed Caroline Herbert, the writer, and they have two sons and a daughter.

The profits from selling his shares in his first two catering ventures were ploughed into his mainstream furniture business, and enabled him to go from a workshop to a factory and buy some furniture-making machinery. He was also importing basketware from Madeira through a company called Basketweave. The ideas were beginning to burst through into commercial projects at an increasing speed.

By 1960 Conran was making contract furniture for Olivetti, and designing the fabric for the P & O liner, the *Canberra*. But he was still dissatisfied with the way that retailers displayed and sold his goods.

Sir Terence has always had a strong sense of what he wants and is determined to get it, which is why his occasional attempts at business partnerships have never lasted long. He realised long before anyone else in this country that the shop where something is sold is as much a part of the product as anything in the product itself.

But in the early 1960s only one shop in London – Woollands of Knightsbridge – was selling his goods in the way he wanted. And the Woollands approach was proving itself: it became Conran's biggest outlet. Conran was so impressed that he used to help out the sales staff on Saturdays and learn from the Woollands formula.

He had already noticed how differently they did things on the Continent, which relatively few British people were visiting regularly at that time. There, it was common for furniture makers to sell to the public directly from their workshops, with all the goods piled up as they came off the production line. Apart from the money it saved, the informality seemed to encourage people to spend. The contrast with the British high street could not have been greater: there, the scene was dominated by large, gloomy stores where the goods were laid out with little or no thought of conveying a coherent view of design.

'It's extraordinary how badly furniture has been sold in this country,' said Sir Terence, 'yet clothes retailing works so much better over here. In those days, the furniture stores were loaded with a huge variety of different styles. They did nothing convincingly.'

There was another motive pushing Conran towards opening his own retail outlets. Shopkeepers generally get their money back as soon as they make a sale. They then sit on it until they have to pay their suppliers, often thirty or sixty days later: the delay varies, depending on the relationship between the two, and who is leaning hardest on whom. To many of the chain stores, Conran would have been just one of a bunch of hopeful, middling-sized furniture makers desperate for some floor space to show off their wares. The others were prepared to put up with that: Conran was not.

There is always a big risk for a manufacturer who decides to sell direct to the public. He suddenly becomes a competitor of his customers. Even if he faithfully sticks to selling only his own output, other retailers will find it hard to avoid the suspicion that if they continued to stock his goods they would actually be paying for someone to take business away from them. Conran, of course, had other ideas. Aside from keeping faith with his own vision of what good-looking furniture ought to be, he would have no inhibitions about buying from makers of other goods which would comple-ment his range.

'Gomme was about the only company that was offering a consis-tent theme with its G-Plan range. In 1964 we were a medium to large furniture manufacturer, but we found it hard to expand because we had to wait for the retailers to pay us. We discovered that as retailers we could expand very quickly indeed. We were convinced that there was a gap in the market. At first we had no idea of going into retailing as such. We just started one shop to show how we would like it done. We already had a showroom, and this was just an extension of that as far as we could see. But having started, we discovered a whole new world. Other retailers told us it would never work outside Chelsea, so we opened our third store in Manchester to see who was right. As it happened, we were, and things just went on from there.'

The first Habitat opened on 11 May 1964 in Fulham. It caused a sensation. The white-painted walls and brown-tiled floors caught the mood and unlocked the purse of fashionable London. The Beatles shopped there, and so did the Royal Family. No retailer could have asked for more. 'It did look very, very, different,' said Sir Terence. 'People used to come and stare.'

It was a repeat of the rapturous reception which had been given to Mary Quant's first Bazaar shop when it had opened in the King's Road, Chelsea, nine years previously. Conran had learned from that success by designing a branch of Bazaar for Quant in 1957. It proved to be an excellent dress rehearsal for Habitat.

What Conran found in 1964, apart from personally becoming an overnight celebrity, was that the store plugged him directly into the shifting whims of his target audience. 'In selling to retailers, we had realised the huge inadequacy of retailers,' Sir Terence recalled. 'Retailing has changed from simply having premises and selecting from various suppliers, to saying this is what we want to sell and we will find the manufacturers to make it to our design.

The retailer has become a much more creative person, largely inspired by the example set by Marks and Spencer. The lead they have given in establishing standards of quality has been very important indeed. Other retailers like ourselves said if they can establish quality, we can lay down other standards. They made it far more interesting to be a retailer.'

Sir Terence admits that his biggest mistake was to merge Habitat with Ryman, the stationers. But it also proved vital in determining the ultimate course of his business career.

After a couple of years' experience with the Habitat shops, Conran decided that he had a business which he could build on. But each shop opening was eating up a lot of capital, and they were absorbing only about fifteen per cent of his furniture manufacturing output. Like many rapidly developing young businessmen, he found that the cash inflow was not fast enough to keep up with his blossoming ambitions.

Just at that moment the Reed Paper Group, as it then was, asked Conran if he would be willing to be taken over. Sir Don Ryder, Reed's chairman in those days, wanted to merge Habitat with his WPM wallpaper shops. Conran, not yet aware of how difficult he would find working for someone else, agreed to the plan. But before it went through, Ryder wanted a feasibility study carried out to examine Habitat's potential. The two companies shared the cost, but it was Conran who got the most out of it because he was able to learn from an outside and dispassionate source exactly what a goldmine he was sitting on.

Reed seemed duly impressed by the weighty volume which emerged from that study. But the deal fell through. Ryder phoned to say that he had decided to take over the International Publishing Corporation instead. Sir Terence admits today that that looks like an excuse: although Reed did indeed take over IPC, that need not necessarily have prevented the Habitat deal. But he has had no reason, then or since, to believe that Reed were other than pleased with the Conran operation.

Whatever thoughts Ryder may have had subsequently, the chance to buy Habitat disappeared because Conran very quickly jumped into a merger with Ryman. 'It was a rapid decision I made on the rebound from Reed,' Sir Terence admitted. 'The Reed negotiations had made us feel very grown-up, talking to people like Sir Don Ryder.'

Conran married in haste and duly repented at leisure. The early enthusiasm on both sides soon evaporated. The Ryman people took to telling Conran what stock to put in the Habitat outlets, and Conran formed the opinion that Ryman was poorly managed and paternalistic towards the staff. In those circumstances, a proper merger of two such distinctive businesses could never really happen. After two years, Conran bought back the Habitat shops, leaving behind his factories, contract showroom, design group and fabric offshoot. It proved to be a turning point.

'The Ryman episode is always painted as a disaster, but it wasn't. It was just that Habitat did not get the attention it deserved. I saw Habitat staying there with a few shops and doing nothing. I decided that it was more important to me to develop Habitat, so I bought it out. Ryman did not see the opportunity for Habitat that I did. However, it was my fault and I have always felt embarrassed about it.'

The name and the shops were all he could buy, because that was all Ryman was offering, and it was probably as much as he could afford. Over half the £670,000 price was met by a loan from Midland Montagu Industrial Finance. But the effect was to focus Conran's attention on what his business was really about: pure retailing.

In the short time he ran it as a combined factory-to-shop operation, he had not entirely escaped the drawbacks of such a strategy. Other manufacturers had been chary of supplying him, fearing he would steal their ideas or leave them high and dry in lean times so that he could keep his own factory busy. And the mixture had muddied Conran's priorities.

'Retailing and manufacturing are uncomfortable bedfellows,' said Sir Terence with the advantage of hindsight. 'They are always out of phase with each other. Manufacturing involves a different side of people, different attitudes. They have to be kept at arm's length, and it's important to have them there to recriminate against.' Nowadays the only manufacturing operations are those that joined the group as part of a bigger acquisition, like Heal's bedding and cabinet factory.

Armed with that sense of identity and purpose, Conran was able to refine the Habitat approach. By the time he went public and merged with Mothercare in 1981 he had boiled that approach down to seven key rules for converting another chain of shops to the Habitat way of life:

1 Market research. Find out what the firm's relationship is with its customers, and what state the business is in.
2 Decide on a design policy for the group. The product is the most important thing of all.
3 Build a design team. Get the right buyers into place. This, according to Sir Terence, can take some time – in the case of Richard Shops, about a year.
4 Study the environment in which the products are going to be sold. Talk to the consumers about what the store should look like, the mood.
5 Put in a programme of refurbishment.
6 Put in the retail systems, stock control and personnel systems.
7 Advertise, to let people know about the changes.

Sir Terence declared: 'The retailing systems are the most important part of the business, perhaps even more important than the design. The point of sale, the stock control, the delivery system, these are what matter. The catalogue is good for us, because it means that people can know when we are out of stock. That makes us try a little bit harder. We are usually five per cent out of stock, whereas most retailers are about fifteen per cent out. You must remember that we buy from all over the world. We have hand-made products from India, which you can expect any time. A flood, a drought, a problem with transport, any of these things can hold up supplies.'

While the problems of an Indian rugmaker might be a cause for concern, the systems which Sir Terence has carefully thought out would be worthless without the right spirit among the staff in the shops and the management who surround him. The Ryman experience made him determined to install a profit-sharing and share incentive scheme which would remove any feelings of 'them' and 'us'. That is reinforced by rigorous staff training. Just in case anyone is in any doubt, the video shown to new recruits is entitled

'Habitat Is Different'.

Among his closest colleagues, Sir Terence seems to inspire a cocktail of undying devotion laced with the feeling that he is hard to get to know. He himself said that the moment he learned to delegate was a watershed.

'All the elements in the business report back into the centre,' he explained, 'but they are very much responsible for their own operations. We try and learn from each part, whether they are doing well or badly. We had a problem in France, and they felt very humbled, felt they ought to do better because they were letting the rest down. But when something like that happens, everyone comes round and tries to help.'

On less fraught occasions, the executives meet regularly to exchange views and criticise one another. Sir Terence believes that it can help if people can vent their feelings in this way.

He decided that the Mothercare merger had given him an insight into the clothing trade. He had also been chairman of Hepworth, the menswear group, and had been responsible for Hepworth launching the highly successful Next chain selling women's co-ordinates in a fresh and distinctive way.

Sir Terence resigned from Hepworth to avoid a conflict of interest in May 1983, and then put together a younger version of Next, called Now. He was aware that Richard Shops might come on the market because it had looked for some time as if its parent, UDS Group, was liable to be taken over. In 1983 Hanson Trust did precisely that.

'We felt ready for Richard Shops,' said Sir Terence. 'What purported to be a management buyout was really a case where four people, the directors, had four per cent of the equity and the institutional funds were being asked to back them. They did not really have enough of a reputation for the institutions' liking. But there was a good group of people there and a fantastic property portfolio. There was enough margin in the property to get the business right.'

That property cushion has given Sir Terence the breathing space to embark on the lengthy task of embedding the Habitat philosophy into everyone at Richards from the managing director down to the newest sales girl. In 1986 he was repeating the process on a much bigger scale in the wake of Habitat Mothercare's merger with British Homes Stores to form a new group called Storehouse.

He declared: 'The key to it all is building a team of people that is persuaded that our ideas are good ideas. In that sense, success breeds success. If we were an unsuccessful firm trying to build something, people would be asking, who do they think they are, trying to tell us what to do? When you are riding high it's easy to persuade people that what you are doing is right. I hope that does not sound too big-headed, because the most important thing is to retain a sense of humility, so that people can approach me with their own ideas.'

Nevertheless, any ideas anyone does put forward must fit in with what Conran sees as the overriding vision of what the company is trying to do. Only in that way will the customer walking into one of the stores have the impression that the whole has been put together by 'one pair of eyes', as he puts it.

'They may say "I don't like coming here", but hopefully they will say "These people have been thinking about what I want",' Sir Terence explained. 'It's a great balancing act between what people's current opinions are and what they might want.'

He is constantly scouring for clues to the great rolling conundrum of public taste. He watches to see what books and newspapers people are reading, and what it is in them that touches a chord. The restaurants and cafés they visit, where they go on holiday, what films and television programmes they choose, and even what sort of a love life they have.

How this is applied depends on the business Sir Terence is looking at. He admits that it is harder to influence the Mothercare audience, partly because they come from such a wide spectrum and partly because many of them have been given firm advice by their mothers before they set off for the shop!

The clarity of the Conran vision is most apparent at Heal's, the family-run department store group which Habitat Mothercare bought in the early part of 1983. The press quickly seized on what they saw as the similarity in outlook between Heal's and Habitat, with the exception that Heal's appealed to an older age group. The standing joke was that Sir Terence must have been afraid that his original trendy young followers were slipping away from him into middle age, and had bought Heal's to offer them something slightly less demanding.

There is some truth in that, as Sir Terence has conceded. But if anyone thought that meant he was going to leave Heal's largely untouched, they were considerably mistaken. Eighteen months after the deal, the sound of a carpenter's hammer still resounded around the main store in London's Tottenham Court Road. Sir Terence has turned the top floor into his own very elegant head office, and the vast amount of spare space has become design and photographic studios for the group. Anything which has detracted from the overriding vision, as seen by the Conran design team, has been removed or modified.

But that, after all, has been the Conran hallmark. It is all of a piece with the early determination not to put up with furniture retailers unsympathetic to his beliefs, and the later refusal to compromise with the conflicting vision of the Rymans. Yet Sir Terence is not widely regarded as a ruthless dictator. That can only mean there is enough room for variation within the overriding vision for others to feel they have a contribution to make, subject to Sir Terence's final verdict.

Certainly, there is enough room in the vision for Sir Terence to try his hand at a growing range of activities, both commercial and philanthropic. In 1981 he sank £2 million into the Boilerhouse Project, a museum of industrial design based in the former boiler-house yard of the Victoria and Albert Museum. His growing collection of early telephones, typewriters and petrol pumps is destined to be moved to an even more ambitious home – a converted dockside warehouse on the south bank of the Thames.

It will be a major attraction of the Butler's Wharf redevelopment Sir Terence is masterminding near Tower Bridge, in conjunction with Jacob Rothschild, the merchant banker, and Alastair McAlpine of the McAlpine building dynasty. Amidst the carefully preserved shells of the old warehouses will be 400 flats, an hotel, theatre, dance centre, workshops, offices, shops and restaurants. Sir Terence will ensure that it is the epitome of late twentieth-century good taste.

Meanwhile, he has linked up with Paul Hamlyn in a publishing venture, and found time to help design a new generation of computers for the Department of Health and Social Security's unemployment benefit offices.

Even Sir Terence's old interest in catering lingers on, through the Neal Street Restaurant in Covent Garden and the in-store café at Heal's. They are a long way, in style and price, from the Soup Kitchens. But there would undoubtedly be a ready market for a Conran restaurant chain, if ever he decided to take it seriously.

Above all, the Conran story demonstrates the power of an idea, if only its creator has the faith and determination to carry it through. It is also a testimony to the strength which some people can draw from being underestimated. 'A sneer pushes you on like anything,' said Sir Terence. 'I remember our bank sneering at Habitat when it started. They thought it was here today, gone tomorrow. And again, there was a slight sneer about Ryman's refusal to see the potential of Habitat.'

A huge personal fortune and a knighthood later, no one is sneering at Sir Terence Conran any more.

Michael Golder

If it were really true that those who can, do, and those who can't, teach, then Michael Golder might still be lecturing polytechnic students on the subject of land economics. He is by no means the only academic to have made the leap into a successful business career, but his is still a rare breed. He comes from Oxfordshire, where his father was a bricklayer and his mother a bus conductress. But by the time he had taken his degree at the London School of Economics he had carved out a secure academic future, and with his soft-spoken manner and fondness for bow ties he could still pass for a slightly other-worldly don. But anyone falling into that assumption would be making a big mistake. After a logical and hardheaded switch of career, Michael Golder now heads one of Britain's fastest-growing catering and leisure groups.

Not many of his customers have heard of the name Kennedy Brookes. Golder is the country's biggest independent restaurateur, but he has built his business through a series of eating chains which have no apparent connection with one another as far as the customer is concerned. They include Mario and Franco, Wheeler's, Genevieve, Maxim's de Paris, a clutch of wine bars in smart corners of London and a handful of country pubs.

The very size of the group has successfully challenged the long-held wisdom that high quality catering cannot be expanded beyond a chain of half-a-dozen outlets or so. Golder and his two key colleagues, Roy Ackerman and Laurence Isaacson, have found a management technique that can be adapted to suit what seems to be an infinite range of variations.

But the transition from common room to boardroom was not straightforward for Golder. It began with a feeling of unease at the prospect of being confined within the walls of an academic institution, and grew to a full-blooded desire to make a substantial fortune.

'I knew I didn't want to lecture all my life,' Golder explained, 'and promotion is so slow in the universities. So I took a consultancy with a firm of stockbrokers in the City. Then it began to dawn on me how unreal academic life is and how frankly ignorant most academics are about the subject on which they are lecturing. It made me rather contemptuous of them. I now notice that in any Government inquiry there is always an academic who has never run anything in his life, but who is supposed to tell everyone how to do it. They always go in for theorising, and they always assume infinite time. You should see the forms they expect me to fill in nowadays! I had to unlearn all that sort of thinking when I went into business for real.'

Armed with this powerful injection of disillusionment, Golder immersed himself more and more in the City and the business world. He graduated from being a consultant to a full-time job as a researcher, and wound up managing a Eurobond fund for Carr Sebag, the former stockbroking firm.

'People sometimes describe me as having been a Eurobond dealer,' said Golder with a smile, 'but the one thing I could never do in the City was deal. I am not the sort of person who has the patience to cope with the cat-and-mouse tactics of buying and selling. I could make the right selections, and knew when to sell them, but the actual dealing I left to others. That's still the case today with Kennedy Brookes.'

He came in contact with the catering business through a company called Roadchef, which among other things operates motorway service stations. He became finance director there, and that was where he met Ackerman, a trained chef. But even this taste of the business world proved insufficient for Golder's growing ambition. 'I enjoyed the City, and I still take a great interest in it,' he said, 'but although you can get paid enormous salaries you can never build up a sizeable capital out of income. To do that, you have to start something yourself and make it work.'

Golder realised that he had to break away on his own. He felt he had two choices: the building trade, stemming from his knowledge of land economics and the quantity surveyors he taught on his course, or making use of the know-how he had garnered from Roadchef to go into catering. 'It had to be a business where there was a low cost of entry and plenty of opportunity. Both fitted the bill, and why I chose restauranting I don't really know, except that you can buy a restaurant and get a mortgage on it fairly easily. On the other hand, the risks were more than I really appreciated at the time.'

By then he and Ackerman were in senior positions at Roadchef, but neither had a significant share stake in the company. 'I wanted my own space,' Golder explained, 'and they did not want to go public, for their own very good reasons. My real reason for leaving was that I wanted to do precisely that, whatever type of business it was in, so that I could make capital. I still feel that I did not make a decision to go into restauranting. I just run a company that happens to be in restaurants. I am very emotionally committed to restaurants, because I am very committed to the company.'

Ackerman persuaded him to sink his annual stockbroker's bonus into buying Kennedy Brookes, a catering firm whose sole outlet was Brookes Restaurant in the Old Brompton Road, near Harrods. It cost £32,000, with the help of a second mortgage on his house. Brookes was a smart hamburger joint at a time – 1973 – when the idea of serving a large and meaty version of the humble hamburger in comfortable surroundings was something of a novelty. In those days the old-style waitress-service Wimpy Bars were the standard. 'The code word then was "American",' Golder recalled. 'If you described your hamburgers as American that meant "not Wimpy".'

Wimpy itself has long since taken the point and upgraded its products to the size and quality of their transatlantic cousins. But when Golder was getting into the business, the rarity value gave him the elbow room to make mistakes whilst charging enough to give him a financial cushion. He needed all of that. 'I learnt all the basics of bulk buying, handling staff and building in stock control systems, in some cases the hard way,' said Golder. 'People think that enthusiasm can make up for a lack of professionalism. It can't.'

He added one or two more outlets, picking up the Fulham Road branch of the Great American Disaster chain and renaming it The American. But before long Golder realised that he would have to expand away from hamburgers. The eating-out market was changing rapidly, especially in London. But from the point of view of anyone in the business of selling hamburgers, 1975 was the year when life would never be the same again: McDonalds arrived in Britain. 'It's one thing to take on a lumbering giant,' Golder pointed out wryly, 'but it's quite another matter to take on a lean, efficient giant who is determined to expand. After McDonalds, there was no way we could be the market leader in that part of the business.'

In fact, the upper end of the burger market retained much of its appeal for people who wanted their taste of the US in a more elaborate form than the McDonalds cartons and did not care to queue for the privilege. This enabled Golder to switch the emphasis of his business in his own good time: he did not sell The American until 1985, and by then he had converted the old Brookes into Hilaire, a sophisticated French restaurant.

In the meantime he diversified into wine bars, which after decades in the doldrums came back into fashion in the 1970s on the back of foreign holidays and rising standards of living, particularly among the growing numbers of working women in the centre of London. The newly affluent young wanted somewhere more congenial than the traditional pubs, many of which were badly in need of a facelift. Besides, the public houses tied to the big brewery groups were committed to pushing beer and spirits across the bar and in the early days found it hard to adapt to the idea of selling bottles of wine for customers to linger over. So Golder opened Blake's in Covent Garden and Daly's in the Strand as the basis of a series of themed London wine bars.

But this market in its turn became overcrowded, and Golder was still searching for a repeatable formula which he could bolt on to a strong brand name. Progress up to now had been steady, but fairly slow. What he lacked was the feel for the business of someone who had been steeped in the catering trade. That gap was filled in 1980 by Golder's colleague from the Roadchef days, Ackerman. He, in the meantime, had launched his own company, Alfresco Feasts, involved mainly in party catering in and around the Oxford area. Alfresco Feasts duly merged with the embryonic Kennedy Brookes.

That gave the group a total of about twenty outlets and the outdoor catering business, which was able to boast the contract for Henley Royal Regatta. They deliberately set about building credibility, with customers, suppliers and particularly with potential financial backers. Golder arranged for Kennedy Brookes' shares to be traded privately among stockbrokers, to get it better known. 'The great thing is take-off,' said Golder, 'take-off in terms of money and reputation in the City, in terms of what you say being believed. Then you can do things, get the business moving. Now, if I say that if we do this, this and this something will work, people say "Here's the money". Before, they didn't.' After seven years of seemingly marking time, within the next three years Golder had pole-vaulted Kennedy Brookes into the big time with a string of shrewd takeovers.

They soon got the measure of their credibility gap when they made their first big takeover play, for Wheeler's the fish restaurant chain which had been an established public company for several years. They were turned down. 'Our offer simply was not treated seriously,' Golder admitted. But that proved to be only a temporary setback. For it was an open secret that an even more attractive name was for sale: Mario and Franco, the chain that had started the fad for white-tiled Italian trattorias back in 1959, and fed the glitterati of the swinging sixties at The Terrazza, Trattoo, Terrazza-Est and Trat-West.

At the height of their fame Mario and Franco floated their company on the stock market, buoyed on a tide of goodwill from their show business and celebrity customers. But they never really cracked the problem of expanding beyond the number of restaurants that the two proprietors could visit between them each day. They got as far as eight in London and opened others in Leeds and Manchester. But Franco died and Mario wanted to sell, so the business was taken over by Spillers, the milling and pet food group best known to the public for its advertisements featuring the little bowler-hatted flour graders.

No one outside the company was ever entirely sure why Spillers wanted to get into the pasta-and-Valpolicella business. The trattorias certainly used flour, but not enough to make any noticeable difference to one of the biggest millers in the land. Before long Spillers became ground down by the competition in the bakery industry and was itself swallowed by Dalgety, an animal feeds company with a decidedly more hard-headed approach to Italian restaurants than Spillers had demonstrated. Dalgety kept Mario and Franco for more than a year while it chalked up trading losses of £300,000, then surprised the trade by selling to Golder for £1.2 million in a mixture of cash and Kennedy Brookes shares.

Golder has described that deal as 'the biggest coup we ever made'. It was literally make or break, for by the time they bought it Mario and Franco was losing money at twice the rate that the rest of Kennedy Brookes was making it. If they could turn it round, their name was made and many more doors would open for them. If they failed to do the trick, Mario and Franco could well have pulled them down with it.

But the conditions were right for Golder. The smart restaurant trade in London was depressed in the summer before the deal. It was 1981, when it took two dollars of an American tourist's money to buy one pound sterling, and many who had been thinking of making the trip had in any case been put off by the Brixton riots a few months previously. Kennedy Brookes' own business at that time did not rely heavily on tourism, and Golder had made the company's shares more attractive to Dalgety and others by upgrading them to the Stock Exchange's Unlisted Securities Market, a staging post on the way to a full listing.

Far from pulling its new parent down, Mario and Franco proved to be the springboard for the important deals which followed. In the next year the group took over the Genevieve chain of five central London restaurants owned by wine expert Joseph Berkmann. It included Locket's, the MPs' restaurant in Westminster, and a stake in the Zanzibar Club. The deal also carried a long-term contract for Berkmann to supply Kennedy Brookes with wine at advantageous prices.

By this time Golder's fast-growing empire was running up sales of more than £10 million a year but making profits of only £600,000. That's the sort of profit margin that supermarkets settle for and restaurants blanch at, but investors accepted that the new acquisitions had to be bedded in and the Kennedy Brookes shares were in steady demand. Golder and Ackerman's ability to tighten cost controls and motivate the staff at Mario and Franco had earned them the respect which brings lucrative deals in its wake. In quick succession they pulled off no fewer than three such trans-actions which set the pattern of the group for the foreseeable future.

The first gave Kennedy Brookes control over the UK rights to the name of Maxim's de Paris, the legendary *fin de siecle* Paris restaurant in the Rue Royale on the edge of the Place de la Concorde. The centrepiece of the franchise deal was to be a London Maxim's fitted out at a cost of nearly £1 million in Panton Street, off Leicester Square, but the rights also allowed Kennedy to market and merchandise goods and run a cookery school under the Maxim's de Paris name. These spinoffs were likely to be more profitable than the gravy from the tables of the restaurant itself, which had a quiet start.

Next, the group won the catering rights for the new Trocadero complex just off Piccadilly Circus. It was an ambitious £3 million scheme, taking the themes of French, Italian and English cuisine and turning them into a series of eating areas ranging from a Mario and Franco trattoria to a French bistro and an English pie shop.

By October 1983 Golder had the clout to go back to Wheeler's and do the deal he had been denied a couple of years before. This time they could not ignore him. After the death of Bernard Wheeler, a huge man who could scoff oysters like some people nibble peanuts, much of the drive and flair had left his famous fish restaurant business. Trade shrank, and in an effort to win back the customers the management cut prices – a mistake, because at that end of the eating-out trade people can afford not to look too closely at the prices. They might jib if the bill is too steep, but tend not to make an extra booking because the lobster is £1.50 cheaper. In any case, a good meal in the right atmosphere is more important than a shaving off the price of the main course. 'I have every sympathy with the problems they faced,' said Golder, 'but over the years they had got away from their traditional menu and started adding things which people nowadays don't always want, like potato piped round the edge of the dish. We took Wheeler's back to its original approach, doing things well but simply, and playing up the health-food aspects of eating fish.'

Golder now had his main building blocks in place. The group was big enough to demand bulk bargain deals on everything from the food and drink to soap powder and cutlery. Central buying in turn gave Kennedy strong control over costs: the small head office team knew what they were paying for supplies, and knew exactly what was being delivered to each outlet. And the group covered a wide enough spectrum not to be caught out by any sudden change of fashion, with a firm base in the central London heartland of the eating-out trade.

But just as he had needed Ackerman to lay the foundation of catering expertise, now Golder realised that he had to have some-one with the marketing experience to exploit the brand names he had accumulated. Once again he turned to an old acquaintance, Laurence Isaacson, whom he had met when they were students at LSE. 'I produced him in a revue we did at college,' said Golder, 'and we kept in touch. I like to deal with people I've known a long time – you don't make so many mistakes that way.' In the mean-time Isaacson had had a successful career in advertising, becoming deputy chairman of a firm called simply The Creative Business. And that was precisely what he started to provide at Kennedy Brookes.

Although the trio of Golder, Ackerman and Isaacson all appear to contribute different skills, they insist that they each dabble in everything. Ackerman has been largely in charge of overseeing the building and decorating of new premises, Isaacson is managing director of the company running Maxim's de Paris, and Golder has developed a keen sense for whether a restaurant idea is working or not. One of the beauties of the trade is that if you have a successful group it is not too expensive to close or modify one branch that is not working to plan. But what Golder is after are styles that can be conjured up into chains which can be packaged and franchised out.

'I want to turn Wheeler's into the British equivalent of McDonalds,' said Golder, 'not in terms of mass-market fast food, but as a name that the world can identify with the best of this country's food. After all, we are an island. If we can't serve up decent fish, who can?' To achieve that dream, he has developed Wheeler's into a form that can be franchised, so that independent caterers can start their own Wheeler's on lines laid down by Kennedy Brookes in return for a royalty. The emphasis of the menus has been shifted towards the growing fashion for lighter dishes, while keeping to the overall theme of sole and lobster. They will all have the same furniture and carpets, whilst leaving room for personal touches at each branch.

There is no reason why this cannot be done with most of the group's successful names, and Golder is constantly experimenting to try and find that elusive blend which is repeatable without being too bland. 'It can be remarkably difficult,' Golder admitted. 'Either a dish will be popular for a few weeks and then suddenly die, or a really good one will be too hard for the chefs to be sure of getting right all the time. After all, it may be just one mistake on the night for him, but for the customer it could be a special anniversary dinner spoiled. It's like a live performance every night, and to make that work as a business you have got to make it as reliable as possible. Everything is about how many customers you get, because of the mark-up on the food and drink. It's quite a small difference that gets you into profit or loss, depending whether you have covered your overheads or not. You have got to have a brand name to pull them in, and a carefully costed menu to make sure that you make your money. Costing a menu is a highly professional job. You can't charge the earth because people soon notice it, even at Maxim's.'

Golder contrasts Kennedy Brookes with the classic rural French restaurant, where the chef goes off to market in the morning and buys enough fresh food for the likely number of covers, and the prices are worked back from there. The local gourmets will accept the resulting menu and prices because he probably went to the market himself that day and knows what was available, and how much it cost.

'We cannot work like that,' Golder explained, 'because in each case we are selling a certain style of restaurant, and the customers have certain expectations. That means we have to produce a balanced menu, regularly repriced to come out at a bill people will not be put off by. So we start off from what we think is the right price and work back – just the opposite of the French approach.' Most of the Kennedy Brookes outlets reprice their menus about three or four times a year, less often at the wine bars where the fare is simpler, but always after the Chancellor's Budget speech.

The selection of the menu is an art in itself. The most popular dishes in London tend to be avocado pear with prawns or crab-meat, steak and apple pie. 'But that would be a pretty boring menu, so you make sure you have other things like smoked fish, say, to make the avocado and the rest look good. People like to feel, if they are going into a reasonably smart restaurant, that they can have the choice of something more sophisticated, even if they still end up ordering the same old thing.' The other vital consideration is to produce a menu which will enable the kitchen to function smoothly: too many dishes that take half an hour to prepare, and the system can grind to a halt, leaving the customers hungrily drumming their fingers on the tables.

One or two of the group's top-of-the-range outlets, such as Hilaire and Lafayette, are allowed to operate in the true French style. The menu changes two or three times a week, and the chef has a fairly free hand to experiment. Those experiments sometimes conjure up dishes which can be put into menus elsewhere in the chain, but the true purpose is to provide flagship restaurants which show that Kennedy Brookes can offer the best. Potential clients for the group's outside catering division are entertained at these haunts, and the main topic of conversation is usually the food itself.

To encourage the general run of customers to feel that they are in good company and also getting privileged treatment, Golder has shrewdly set up in-house cards and club deals in the leading chains, including Maxim's. Mario and Franco has an outlet called The Club in Belgravia, and there is also the Zanzibar Club, a cocktail bar near Drury Lane.

Members are offered special menus and special themed nights are laid on, as well as fixed-price meals combined with tickets for top West End shows. This is an excellent way of building up goodwill and encouraging members to keep using the restaurants. But equally valuable to Golder is the fact that the 15,000 members in the group constitute a very useful mailing list and a constant source of market research evidence about those members' likes and dislikes. The mailing list is of course an ideal advertising medium for any new Kennedy Brookes ideas.

'We want people to enjoy themselves in our restaurants,' Golder explained, 'and that goes for the staff as well as the customers. The staff have to be kept interested or they get slack, and of course you want the customers to keep coming back.' So Golder keeps things on the move. Promising managers are switched from one site to another, and new attractions are regularly laid on to maintain the customers' interest. Italian opera was introduced at the Terrazza-Est in Chancery Lane to enliven quiet Monday trade. It was successful enough to make it into a nightly event. But if it had flopped, it would have cost nothing to drop the idea. Said Golder: 'I am a great believer in the need to have an identity, to have something unique. You can make all sorts of mistakes, but people who have made a lot of money have had some sort of exclusivity.'

But all the exclusivity in the world will count for nothing if the costs are not controlled and the money counted in. 'The overwhelming thing is work,' Golder admitted. 'Things do not just go right. People assume there is a magic formula you can plug into. There isn't. One certainty in this business is that you are going to get things wrong, and you have to be there to correct mistakes. You must do something about it. I am more impressed when I see what people do when they are in a hole. How they get themselves out is the most crucial element.'

The group is run by a small head office team of about eleven, who between them take responsibility for everything from future strategy to central buying. 'Our control systems are robust and practical, rather than sophisticated,' said Golder. 'I believe that collecting figures is not in itself useful. Everything must be judged on whether it helps to sustain or make a decision. We concern ourselves with the overall profit margins, the costs and the buying prices. But if you want to check what's selling and what isn't, it's cheaper to do a manual survey of bills than set up some amazing computer program. When we took it over, Mario and Franco's accounting system was far better than ours, but the results were terrible.'

Ackerman supervises the design and fitting out of new restaurants, while Golder tends to think of himself in City terms as the head of a corporate finance department. But both of them share with Isaacson a feel for the marketing side of the business. One of their golden rules is that location is the most important factor in the success of any restaurant, wine bar or café.

'When you've got a first-class site, not even poor management can kill it,' Golder claimed. He has taken this principle to its logical conclusion by acquiring one of the most prominent buildings on arguably the most famous roundabout in the world, the London Pavilion at Piccadilly Circus. It was a cinema which lay empty for several years until Kennedy Brookes bought it in 1984 for £2.5 million and planned to spend another £10 million on installing a range of restaurants and entertainments.

Sums like that trip off the tongue of an entrepreneur all too easily, but Golder has manoeuvred himself into deals of this size by going in for joint ventures. Kennedy Brookes' involvement in the Trocadero and the London Pavilion deal have been achieved by setting up separate companies in which Kennedy Brookes has a controlling 51 per cent stake. In some cases the partners have been trade associates such as Young and Co., the brewers, or James Burroughs, the Beefeater gin firm. Other schemes have been set up with private investors. While this approach can leave the main company open to conflicts of interest, it does enable Golder to put his hands on much more ambitious projects than he would otherwise be able to get near. Of course, it is a virtuous circle: the bigger the deal he can pull off, the bigger the next one.

Kennedy Brookes is rapidly bursting out of its original restaurant concept and coming closer to being an all-round leisure group. Golder makes no secret that he would like to apply his techniques to hotels and maybe even American-style theme parks. Kennedy Brookes has an interest in a travel agency, which is another potential avenue. Why not arrange for a trainload of Maxim's well-heeled patrons to take a trip on the Orient Express?

The possibilities for the group are endless, so long as Golder and his two partners can keep an eye on everything at once. But that necessity could in itself prove a critical turning point for Kennedy Brookes. Golder has until now determinedly kept the company on a scale which the ruling trio can manage by themselves. But companies acquire a dynamic of their own, and Golder's next challenge will be to decide how to build a system which will enable him to keep control without stopping the flow of new ideas. The alternative will be to succumb to one of the regular takeover offers which are floated across his desk by the giants of the leisure industry. 'But if that happens,' he said, 'the three of us will just leave. We don't want to work for anyone else.'

All three have service contracts with the group running into the early years of the next century, and can be cut short only on five years' notice. If an unfriendly takeover predator wanted Golder out immediately, the compensation could run to more than £150,000. That in itself is a minor consideration, set against Golder's share stake in Kennedy Brookes, worth in the region of £2 million.

Yet even now Golder claims that he has never reached the point where he felt financially secure. 'Being a millionaire is just not what it was,' he said, 'when you think that there must be dozens of houses in London worth half a million. You would probably need £50 or £60 million to be as well off as a millionaire before the war.'

Unlike some other entrepreneurs, Golder has not let his success alter his lifestyle. He lives in the same house he had before the business took off and relaxes in a modest way. 'I go skiing in the winter,' he said, 'but I stay in a plain, ordinary chalet like everyone else. I suppose what I'd really like to do is spend a month in China, but I can't get away for that long at a time. Naturally I eat quite well, but I always did, even when I couldn't afford it. I never felt poor when I was poor, and I don't feel rich now that I am rich.'

But Golder does enjoy one luxury that is confined to the very wealthy: making money has become more of a game and less a matter of earning enough to pay the rent. 'I want to make a £5 million profit instead of £2 million,' he explained, 'simply because five beats two.'

Harry Goodman

In the past quarter of a century, the travel trade has been a cockpit for the young buccaneers – and quite a few cowboys – of the business world. At the start it was easy to get in, and even easier to get a bloody nose. Sleepy Spanish fishing villages mushroomed into holiday playgrounds as the new British tour firms fought to fill the beaches with crowds of customers paying rock-bottom prices for sun, sand and Rioja.

Today the cowboy days are over. Several well-publicised scandals, notably the collapse of Clarksons in 1974, saw to that. Now the tour operators have to be licensed, and have to put up a bond to compensate stranded holidaymakers in the event of financial failure. The industry has gone through the classic cycle of spawning hundreds of small firms which are being remorselessly whittled down to a handful of large groups run on professional lines.

The most colourful of the survivors to make the big time is Harry Goodman. A fast-talking, out-going trader who enjoys the private yacht and plane that a multi-million fortune puts within reach, his career spans virtually the entire history of the package tour trade. He left school at the age of fifteen in 1954, only to be turned down for a job by Thomas Cook, the doyen of Britain's travel agents, because he had no 'O' Levels. Now he is chairman of International Leisure Group, which includes Intasun, Global Holidays and Club 18–30 and takes more than a million people a year to the snow or sand that tell most Brits they are on holiday.

'When I left school I tried to get into the travel business because to me travel meant getting on planes, and that's what I wanted to do,' Goodman said as he relaxed in his house off the King's Road in Chelsea. 'Now I'm in a position where if I stopped enjoying the business, I would get out. I don't think you have to become successful by treading on people.'

But in the early days Goodman certainly had to use his elbows to find a corner for himself. His father, an East End sewing machinist, died when Harry was only two, and he was orphaned when he was eleven. He was brought up by a family friend until he was old enough to live on his own. 'I always wanted to run my own business,' he recalled. 'I couldn't work for anyone else.'

That was easier said than done, at first. After the Thomas Cook rejection, Goodman settled for a clerking job with the Co-op in Lehman Street, Whitechapel. Eventually a persuasive old aunt got him into a travel agency in Hatton Garden because the manager lived next door to her. Ironically it was called Thompson's Travel, a near namesake for the holidays giant that was to become Goodman's great rival.

Two years of National Service and another humdrum job later, the budding tycoon was still making little progress. 'Then I saw an advert in *Travel Trade Gazette* for something called the Travel Saving Association, backed by the Union Castle and P & O shipping lines,' said Goodman. 'It was based on door-to-door selling, and of course the two backers started it up mainly so that they could fill their ships. But they also had an air travel department, and I talked my way into the job of running that for them. I didn't know anything about it, but I recruited people who had worked in air travel – and I became a great delegator!'

That went on for about four years, before the inevitable happened. Union Castle and P & O fell out and closed the whole thing down. Goodman was out of work, 22 and still broke.

But by this stage the package holiday business was starting to take off. It was the early 1960s, the Costa Brava was opening up, and there were plenty of opportunities. Travel firms were continually changing hands, and in 1966 the near-penniless Goodman, with a couple of partners, managed to buy their way into a small Kent-based outfit called Sidcup Travel. It cost them £500 each, and Goodman had to sell his house and move his family into a flat over the business.

Half the shop was a jewellers when they took it over, so they painted the jewellery counter and used that as the counter for the travel agency. But Goodman had other ideas. Before long he had renamed the firm Sunair and was branching out into becoming a tour operator in his own right. 'I thought this door-to-door idea was a good one,' Goodman explained. 'So I put together a programme of holidays and tried to sell them door-to-door. I only sold 1,600 holidays and must have worn out twenty pairs of shoes that year!'

After that experience Goodman returned to the traditional method of selling his holidays through travel agents, a principle he has stuck to ever since. He rapidly emerged as the dominant member of the trio who owned Sunair. 'I was a workaholic,' Goodman recalled, 'and in the end I just had to have control so that I could get things done.' But as he admits, he was very much riding by the seat of his pants at the start.

'In those days I just got other people's brochures and worked the prices back from there,' he explained. 'The hoteliers didn't worry who I was: they would take all the bookings they could, so that they could build the hotels. Hoteliers in Spain at that time were just people who owned a bit of ground by the beach. That's why they would double and triple book, so that they could be sure of getting the money in to pay the builder. It was a new industry, and I would say that everyone in it at that time was a disaster. I had never run a business in my life, and we were all like that. There was no government licensing. You just printed a brochure and hoped it would work out all right.'

By 1971 the big travel groups were taking a serious look at the money being made out of the mass transfer from the British coastal resorts to the Spanish costas. Cunard, another name from the golden era of cruise liners, decided to dip its toe into the new business and bought control of Sunair for £200,000. Goodman stayed on as managing director, but within a few months Cunard itself was taken over by the rapidly expanding Trafalgar House. Goodman decided to strike out on his own again.

Instead of diving straight back into the business, he awarded himself a two-year sabbatical which he used to lay the foundations of what eventually became the present-day Intasun organisation. He had £70,000 from the Sunair sale, and kept himself afloat by starting an employment agency, then a relatively easy way to make money for anyone in the know. At any rate, it was sufficiently trouble-free for him to be able to spend much of his time abroad.

He said: 'I spent those two years travelling in Spain and Greece, building contacts, talking to hoteliers, seeing what could be done. That taught me the fundamentals of the business. I decided we would refuse to pay forward deposits, a policy we have followed ever since we started Intasun. We would never choose numbers for the sake of numbers. We would take as much of the risk out as possible, and that meant contracting hotels and aircraft without commitment. We would never get reliant on owning our own supply of hotels or aircraft. Eventually we did own aircraft, but we have always kept our in-house supply below what we needed.'

Deposits were a legacy of the days of double-booked hotels, when tour operators would put their money down in an attempt to show the hoteliers they were serious and spare their customers from being left out in the street. By not toeing that particular line, Goodman kept the money in his company's coffers, giving it several months' interest and boosting the balance sheet.

Forward commitments were another attempt by the tour firms to ward off their rivals' incursions at the height of the season. But such commitments added to the risks in a business which works on razor-thin profit margins at the best of times.

With those golden rules at the back of his mind, Goodman returned to the UK travel scene. He had his sights on Intasun, a small chain of travel agencies owned by a dentist Goodman knew. He explained: 'When I was ready to get back into the business I wanted to buy a going concern, complete with licences, to save time. He wanted £25,000, which I couldn't raise, so I offered him 25 per cent of the business and the rest in instalments, but he wouldn't agree. If he had, he would have been a multi-millionaire today.'

In the end, Goodman got the money from Derek and Eddie Garcia, two brothers who ran Adda International, a public company which owned a chain of hotels in central London. They gave Goodman a £25,000 debenture loan in return for 9.9 per cent of the company. He bought them out at par three years later.

The first thing Goodman did when he got his hands on Intasun was to sell the three travel agencies to British Caledonian's Blue

Sky chain. He wanted to supply the travel agency trade, and was determined to stay on his side of the fence rather than be accused of competing with his customers.

He made a point of bringing in top people for his senior executive posts, Stephen Matthews, the finance director, came from Charterhouse Japhet, the City merchant bank. Sales director Mike Prior had previously been with the British Eagle airline. These two had teamed up with Goodman after he broke away from Sunair. Peter Woodward, the chief accountant, was picked up from Cranfield Business School. And Sidney Perez, one of the most experienced men in the travel business, was poached from Horizon Travel.

Normally any business starting from scratch like that takes several years to build up a momentum before it can reach take-off speed and begin to grow rapidly. But almost within a year Intasun had a break that most young companies can only dream about, even though it was at the expense of a competitor.

The dominant force in the package tour business of the early 1970s was Clarksons. It carried about a million passengers a year, about the same number as Intasun and Thomson Holidays handle nowadays. But the package holiday market has more than doubled in the meantime. In its heyday Clarksons had nearly half the business to itself. It had increased the traffic by slashing prices, often giving itself a profit margin of as little as 50p per holiday booked. The sheer volume of Clarksons' business gave it an unrivalled edge in bargaining with hoteliers, but it could not afford to let that volume slip or the whole pack of cards would come tumbling down: profit margins would vanish, and the hotels would shut their doors to the firm.

In August 1974 that was precisely what happened. But although it came as a shock to the general public, rumours about Clarksons had been flying around the trade for some years beforehand. Goodman reacted by embarking on a ruthless strategy designed to take full advantage of any collapse.

He recalled: 'We hired and put on standby three private jets and a buying team. We had them airborne forty minutes after the announcement that Clarksons was in trouble. The hoteliers panicked. We got reductions of forty per cent on room rates because we could assure them that their beds would be filled. We brought out a new brochure that was to all intents and purposes Clarksons'. It happened in August, late in the season, but we picked up 50,000 holidays and made £300,000 in the remaining eight weeks of the season.'

That effectively doubled Intasun's business for that summer. Just as important, of course, was the fact that there were a million people who would be looking for someone else to take them on holiday in 1975 and beyond. It was a vacuum which the surviving operators eagerly jumped into.

By this time Harry Goodman was beginning to move into over-drive. It was commonplace for him to leave home at six in the morning and return at midnight, exhausted. And that was when he was not haring around the resorts, trying to make sure that everything was going according to plan for that summer whilst simultaneously planning the programme for the following season.

The business works in a curious kind of time warp. In January or February of year one the operators begin to make their preliminary calculations for the summer of year two, the best part of eighteen months away. The brochures for year one have been on sale long enough for the companies to know what hotels and holiday ideas went down well and what did not. They peer through half-closed eyes into the crystal ball containing the currency rates and overall economic climate for year two, and the broad decisions start to take shape.

How far should they alter the current season's brochure? What new resorts should be introduced, old ones dropped? Should they offer coach travel as well as the ubiquitous charter plane? And should flights be taking off from any new UK airports? In recent years Cardiff, Newcastle, Bristol, Glasgow and others have been used to save holidaymakers the train journey to Luton or Gatwick.

It may be worth making a pitch for minorities, such as the very old or the very young – International Leisure now owns both Golden Days and the frenetic Club 18–30. How about activity holidays? The numbers are small, but people may be prepared to pay more to spend a fortnight pursuing their hobbies. Or they may prefer to spend the same amount of money on a shorter stint at the easel or the bridge table.

In the early summer, one or two holidaymakers may notice that the person next to them is dressed slightly more soberly than everyone else, and may not be tucking into the duty-free drinks with quite the same enthusiasm. The odds are that that is one of the negotiators employed by the tour operators to bargain for room space next year.

If they manage to steer clear of the liquor on the way out there, they are probably glad of a stiff drink by the time they fly home. Under strong pressure from the likes of Harry Goodman to return with the right result, they not only have to haggle with the proprietors of the chosen hotels, they have to fight off rival bids from the representatives of the other tour firms, German and Scandinavian as well as British. The hotelkeepers, of course, try to play one off against the other.

The game does not begin from square one every year. Relationships have developed over the past two decades, and people on both sides know who can be relied upon and what leeway there is on pricing and bookings. But every season brings its own new twist. One year the Germans may be staying at home, or there may be a sudden rush to a new resort. 'That's where experience really tells,' said Goodman.

Once the hotels have been lined up, another poker game begins. The operators must match their bookings with a schedule of flights which will fill and empty the hotels at the right time. By the end of August the horse-trading ends and the brochures for the following summer go to the printers.

One way to cut out the second round of headaches is for the tour firms to have their own airlines. A battle has raged in the industry over whether or not this is a good idea. Doing so naturally helps to solve the problem of matching the planes to the resorts, but a fleet of modern aeroplanes can be a nasty financial albatross if they are not working flat out and bulging at the seams throughout the busy season.

By 1978, although his co-directors were unconvinced, Goodman had no doubts: 'We had to have an airline, because there were so few airlines about who could supply the charter market. There was either Dan-Air or our own competitors among the tour operators, and they could switch off the supply any time they chose. So we started Air Europe, the first new airline for sixteen years. We took the top two guys from Dan-Air, Errol Cossey and Martin O'Regan, and gave them a slice of the equity.'

That was all very well, but Goodman then found himself with an uphill task to persuade a planemaker to sell any planes to Intasun, and an even harder job to find a bank anywhere in the world that would lend the money. The reluctance was understandable: apart from the fact that hardly anyone outside the package holiday trade had heard of Intasun, three planes of the sort they wanted were going to cost £18 million. Intasun's net assets were just £1 million.

Goodman recalled: 'We decided that the Boeing 737 was the aircraft for us. All we could put into the airline was £250,000. Boeing were not interested, so I decided to phone their chairman in Seattle. After all, it wasn't going to cost me anything if he refused to take the call. But I got straight through, which is more than would happen over here. I said to him, "Do you want to sell aircraft or don't you?" They put a team over to us in 48 hours, and they went through our business for three weeks. We came up with a deal where, if we could borrow the money they would take the first twenty per cent of any guarantee to the banks. That meant that if we went bust, Boeing would pay the first 20p in the pound back to the banks.'

But if Goodman had worn out plenty of shoe leather selling his first ever holidays at Sunair, he was to wear out a lot more trying to find the finance for a plane. 'The City of London laughed the idea out of court,' he recalled. 'We went to sixty banks in London, and got thrown out of every one. There was no such thing as risk finance on aircraft in those days, because the banks were used to dealing with state-owned airlines.'

In the end Intasun had to go to Marubeni Corporation of Japan, who would have been well aware that they were not the first port of call for a medium-sized British company with no previous dealings in the Far East. They lent the money, but charged a hefty six per cent over the London inter-bank interest rates for the privilege.

That meant that Goodman had to run very fast indeed to keep up with interest payments of around £2.5 million a year. But he did it with something to spare. 'After paying the interest we made £2 million in the first two years, on three planes,' he said. 'Mind you, we were competing using brand new planes, and that's a big advantage in terms of fuel economy and greater comfort. Aside from carrying Intasun's passengers, we have stayed at the top end of the charter market, hiring the planes out to small operators whose customers don't mind paying the extra quid or two for a more comfortable seat. The other big benefit of owning our own was that aircraft are an incredible tax shelter.'

Air Europe's planes took off in 1979, just as the arrival of a Conservative government, higher interest rates and a surge in North Sea oil production sent the pound soaring. Although dearer interest was not good news for the group, a strong pound made foreign holidays ever more attractive while keeping down the bill for aircraft fuel, as it is priced in US dollars.

The dramatic fall of the dollar against the pound in Margaret Thatcher's first year also opened up a possibility which had hitherto been only a dream for most people in Britain: cheap trips to America. While this led to a vicious round of price-cutting on no-frills flights to New York, package holidays seemed a tall order simply because it was not something the US hotel chains were used to. Until Harry Goodman got the bit between his teeth, that is.

He insisted: 'We started the boom in British holidaymakers going to Miami in 1980, even though Sir Freddie Laker claimed the credit. We were looking around for somewhere new after Spain, and Miami stood out like a sore thumb. In the summer there were mile upon mile of luxury hotels there, with no people in them. I decided we would have to get the prices the same as in Spain. We wanted to pay $10 for a seafront room for two people. We went to every hotel, and they all threw us out. But we needed just one break, and one guy said to us he thought it might work. He didn't want to come in with us, though: he wanted to stand aside and pick up all the South American business which would be driven out of the other hotels if they started taking British packages. So he introduced us to hoteliers who might be persuaded to take our deal, and he gave them the impression that he was already in on it. That did it. We bought 3,000 beds at £2 a night.'

But Intasun's 737s had nothing like the range for the London–Miami run, so Goodman had to strike a deal with someone who had spare planes capable of crossing the Atlantic. Who should be standing there but the now legendary Freddie Laker, who had been busy capturing the headlines with his £99 flights to New York. Goodman said: 'I wanted a DC10 ten times a week, on the basis of £120 a seat for the round trip. Freddie said we were mad, and made us put the money up front. It was a forward commitment of £20 million, breaking our usual rule. But the result was that we could offer a week's holiday in Miami for £179. Before us the cheapest was £350.'

With that touch of showmanship that seems to be an indispensable part of the leisure industry, Goodman fed word of his coup to the BBC's Holiday programme, who obligingly ran the item as a news flash on the Sunday night. The next morning people were queuing outside the Intasun offices. That was in October 1979, and they had sold out their entire stock of 80,000 Miami holidays by November.

Although the Miami hoteliers might have been less than happy at being hustled so comprehensively by Harry Goodman, they cheered up when Intasun spelt out to them the hidden joys of supplying the British holidaymaker, such as the profits on three meals a day plus much fatter bar takings.

'We had to retrain them to cope with British holidaymakers, who expect three meals a day in the hotel, complete with bar and night club,' Goodman pointed out. 'In Miami, they were used to people staying for a couple of nights and moving on, not eating or drinking at all in the hotel. The bar was usually just a few bottles set up in the corner of the lounge. At one place, they had just one barman to serve an 800-bed hotel. We soon put that right, and the hotels adapted very well. After all, they could see the money rolling in if they got themselves organised, couldn't they?'

Short-lived as it proved to be, the American venture turned out to be a landmark for Intasun. 'We made £3 million out of Miami that year,' Goodman said. 'It was one of the deals that really made us because it brought our name to public notice. Freddie always claimed it as his own because he put a few of his own customers into our spare seats on the plane. But Freddie got too greedy, and put our rates up for the planes once he saw it was a success. He hadn't realised that by then all the airlines were scrambling to get in on the act, and we had our pick of the alternatives. In the end we did a plane-swapping deal with Air Florida, using their planes in the summer and letting them have two of ours in the winter.'

Goodman was to cross Sir Freddie Laker's path again in February 1982, but under very different circumstances. They met at Gatwick Airport, where Sir Freddie's bankers and accountants were trying to come up with a last-minute deal which would save Laker Airways from going into receivership. It was to prove a fateful meeting for both men.

'I had made a bid for Laker in October 1981,' Goodman explained, 'but the Midland Bank did not even reply to my letter.' Four months later, on Thursday, February 4, he was contacted in the middle of a business trip to Madrid: Laker Airways was on the verge of collapse, and would Intasun be interested in buying it?

After talks lasting right through the night, Goodman offered £10 million for the two Laker tour firms, Arrowsmith and Laker Air Travel. The bankers were not interested. They wanted a buyer for all or nothing. The meeting broke up at 4 a.m., a receiver was called in and the tour firms were sold separately within a week – for a total of just £5 million.

The main reason for the price halving so quickly was that in the meantime Goodman had stage-managed a repeat of his Clarksons swoop. His Gatwick talks had told him all he needed to know about Laker's hotel bookings for the coming summer. On the morning of the collapse, two Intasun jets took off for Spain with a team of negotiators abroad. They simply went to the hotels in the Laker brochures and asked the crestfallen managers if they had 'any spare beds'.

By the beginning of the following week Intasun claimed to have picked up 50,000 former Laker holidays. They were not alone: a week later Thomas Cook estimated that as many as 90,000 of the 120,000 holidays Laker had arranged for the coming summer had been pocketed by rival tour firms.

The Laker crash marked another watershed for Goodman. Intasun had gone public on the Unlisted Securities Market nearly a year before, but Goodman's unruly hairstyle and flamboyant lifestyle at that time was a little on the wild side for some of the City's more cautious souls. The shares were floated at 91p but fell in the next few months to only 69p as doubts persisted about the group's ability to ride the ups and downs of the holiday trade when it had those cash-eating planes to cope with.

However, in the aftermath of the Laker collapse Intasun sold more than 500,000 holidays in a single summer for the first time, giving it the base to become the industry's second biggest operator. From there it had the clout to buy other operators. It picked up Schoolplan, the ski firm, and Club 18–30, and by 1985 was providing more than a million holidays a year.

Goodman, meanwhile, had toned down his image and begun to hand over day-to-day control over the business to the younger men pushing up through the ranks. In the process, he has had time to think – and to turn some of his earlier ideas on their head.

He said: 'It's taken me three years to disengage, and I'm only just getting used to it. The job cost me my first two marriages, and I missed out completely on family life. I spend six to eight weeks at a time away from the business nowadays, enough to see the wood for the trees. Now I have to learn to walk past meetings as I go down the corridor – although I'm always jumping in afterwards, wanting to know what went on! I still make all the major decisions; I have a lot of ideas. But then, everyone who runs a company has to be autocratic. You cannot run away from decisions. You cannot do it by committee, because a committee never makes decisions in any positive sense. There has got to be a boss. When the going gets tough, someone has got to say "This is what we're going to do".'

Intasun's two biggest decisions, to start Air Europe and go into Miami, were forced through by Goodman against the total opposition of the rest of the board. 'I was overruled by the board seven to one both times,' Goodman remembered, 'but each time we went ahead and did it. I convinced them, and you can get away with that so long as you don't do it too often – and so long as you are right. Mind you, the way I convinced them was to say that if the company does not do this, I will do it on my own. After all, in both instances there would have been no conflict with the company. I wouldn't have been competing with them. In the light of that information, the board changed its decision.'

In 1984 Goodman began to take his board through a U-turn on two major policies. Air Europe was broken up, and the company began to move seriously into hotels. He explained: 'One of the toughest moves I made was to halve the assets of Air Europe. In the year to March 1983, Air Europe made £7 million. We decided in 1984 that the market was going into a downturn for five years. We looked at the rate of return against replacement value. The dollar at the end of the 1984 summer season was 1.20 to the pound. We had written down the planes to £2 million. We sold five of them for £10 million each.' But the cost was that Errol Cossey, one of the two men who had helped Goodman to start Air Europe, walked out.

The move into hotels is part of a strategic shift in the direction of International Leisure. Goodman realises that the City finds it difficult to get away from the idea of the travel industry being risky, hotly as he denies it. So he is adding bricks and mortar to the mixture. 'The travel business is treated differently from other businesses,' he conceded, 'but it's no more risky than the others. I would never take any deal that would put our business at risk. I think our company should be a major international group in five years' time. It will be big in hotels, both here and overseas.'

In the first few months of 1985 he began to move towards those goals. International Leisure bought Global Holidays, which expanded the group's coach traffic, but also gave it a foothold in the Australian market. As a bonus, Global owned two hotels in Majorca.

'The City wants us to do deals,' he confirmed. 'We will, but we will take our time. We went public in 1981 to guarantee the personal security of the main directors. We have seven millionaires in the company. We actually do our homework. We are not lucky. We agonise over our decisions. All the mistakes were made in the early years. We evaluate everything.'

Harry Goodman, who is now so rich he gives his entire yearly salary to charity, is about to face an important crossroads in his career and that of his company. He wants to shift Intasun's centre of gravity to give it a broader base in the leisure industry and so make it less vulnerable to the squalls that blow through the package holiday trade. After twenty years of unstoppable growth there are signs that everyone who wanted to go to Palma or Benidorm has been. It is increasingly an under-30's market, and growth has slowed to five per cent a year at most.

The over-30s are seeking new destinations and demanding more scope for individual freedom on their annual jaunt. And if they are no longer willing to be parcelled up and ferried from bar to bull ring to night club, then it is simply harder to make money out of them. That is why Goodman wants a stake in the accommodation that people have to have: hotels, certainly, and also villas and caravan sites. But it is hard to escape the feeling that there will always be a part of International Leisure which is driven by the seasonal migration of the British holidaymaker in search of sun, sand and duty-frees.

James Gulliver

James Gulliver would be many people's idea of the pugnacious Scot. He is short, stocky and very determined. Ask him when he felt most hard done by in his business career, and he will almost certainly reply that it was on the two occasions when he struck out on his own and was forced to accept restrictions on his freedom of action. In short, for a set period each time he was not allowed to do what he knew he was best at: food retailing.

Although they do not rankle today, those curbs did at the time tell him that he was making an impact on his chosen killing ground. Associated British Foods, the Sunblest bread group, and RCA of America were obviously sufficiently impressed with the budding Gulliver to want to shackle him for a while.

It must have seemed a long way from the three grocer's shops his father ran in Campbeltown, Argyllshire. One has since been demolished, the second is now a hairdresser's and the third has been taken over by one of Gulliver's present-day customers and competitors in the off-licence trade.

Now he runs Argyll Group, named partly to commemorate his homeland, but also for the hard-headed reason that it comes near the top of any alphabetical list. At the time of writing, it takes in more than 1,000 food stores, supermarkets and freezer centres trading under the names of Presto, Liptons, Templeton, Galbraith, Lo-Cost and Cordon Bleu. The group makes Scotch and Bourbon whiskies, rum, gin and vodka as well as tea and biscuits. Yet Argyll was assembled virtually from scratch in the remarkably short time of less than six years, starting with the takeover of Louis C. Edwards, an ailing Manchester butcher, in 1979.

For someone who can properly claim to be a fully-fledged entrepreneur, Gulliver took an unusually long time to find and establish undisputed control of his master company. He was 47 when he did the Edwards deal. Until then, his career had been marked by a good managerial record, flashes of brilliance and a high degree of foresight, but also a readiness to surrender his independence which some of his entrepreneurial peers would scorn. 'Though I always had the drive to do so, I now think I waited too long to start on my own,' he admitted.

He was bright enough to go to university on a scholarship, and he had already begun to think in terms of what would best prepare him for a career in business. He was good at mathematics, but studied engineering because it combined the analytical training with a practical application which might stand him in good stead later. His first-class degree earned him a Fulbright Scholarship to the US: he used that to study at Harvard Business School.

After winning a Royal Navy commission in an otherwise 'frustrating' National Service, and a spell with a small Scottish engineering company, Gulliver decided to spend the next five years as a management consultant with Urwick Orr.

He explained: 'It was a growing business, management consultancy. British industry was just waking up after the war. It was a production-orientated society then. Demand was such that if you could make it, you could sell it. So there was a desire on the part of management to learn new techniques. Over five years, up to 1965, I told other people how to run their companies though I had never actually run one myself.'

But he had made up his mind from the start that five years would be enough. 'After that you do tend to become institutionalised, you possibly stop learning,' he said. 'If you are going to make it into senior line management, that is the time you make your move. When I was joining, I advised Urwick Orr's selection panel that I would only stay for five years. Everyone else was saying they would stay for ever, so it caused a few raised eyebrows. But it was the right thing to do.'

But again, Gulliver postponed the moment of starting his own business, opting instead to do a management job for someone else. 'I wanted a job as a managing director,' he explained. 'I was 33 and had a certain amount of cheek, if you like. I was determined that, however small the company, I would run it and build it.' The job he got was with the Fine Fare supermarket chain, part of the giant Associated British Foods group. But even then he nearly missed what turned out to be the chance of a lifetime. 'The interview was fixed for New Year's Day,' Gulliver recalled, 'which was not a holiday in England at that time. I thought that I wouldn't bother to go, but when I phoned up to cancel the interview the secretary said: "You should come. You've got a good chance of getting the job." So I travelled on Hogmanay to attend that interview – quite a sacrifice for a Scot!'

At this point his career took off. His job was to run the shop-fitting subsidiary of Fine Fare, which had for him the advantage of being away from the mainstream of the business, leaving him a fair amount of autonomy. But he quickly discovered that he was presiding over a hitherto hidden disaster area. The shopfitting company had overstated its profits by £450,000. Within three weeks he was in the office of the late Garfield Weston, then head of Associated British Foods, to spell out exactly how desperate the position was. Weston's reaction was to make Gulliver managing director of the whole of Fine Faire.

'He was ultra-decisive, perhaps with a tendency to overreact,' Gulliver said of Weston. 'Because he was a hands-off entrepreneur he relied entirely on delegation and people he believed in. So he saw this as an opportunity to pull someone who had impressed him – and I think I had – into the group.' Although it was a golden opportunity for Gulliver at the age of 33, Weston was also handing him something of a poisoned chalice. Fine Fare was losing about £2,000,000 that year, and Gulliver was the fifth managing director in seven years. Yet two years later he was chairman of Fine Fare and a director of the parent company, ABF.

The trouble was that Fine Fare was unprofitable and had severe balance sheet problems. Borrowings had gone up to fund losses. Trading had gone down and stocks had built up. Gulliver quickly realised that he had to get the cash moving and stem the losses, then get a good flow of information to improve management decision-taking.

It was an exciting time to be in that business. Supermarkets were only just beginning to get going. The multiple chains' share of the grocery market was about 25 per cent, compared with over seventy per cent today. The stock market was beginning to realise that the supermarkets had enormous potential. In the late 1960s, instead of Fine Fare being a drag on the group, ABF's shares went up because the company owned a supermarket chain.

'I developed Fine Fare as a national company,' said Gulliver. 'It had had 25 separate fascias, around the country, so I introduced a national trading name and logo. We were then able to have own brands and national press advertising. We were the first to do so. Tesco did very little advertising then, and Sainsbury said they would never advertise. But then they did not have supermarkets in those days; they had what they called self-service stores. When I took over at Fine Fare over half the stores were counter service. But self-service went hand-in-hand with a lower wages bill. When a counter service store was converted to self-service, wage costs were often halved. That was a tremendous increase in productivity, and provided us with a major opportunity to improve profits.'

Gulliver stayed seven years as chairman and chief executive of Fine Fare, building the value of the business from £12 million to about £60 million. But then the rules of the game changed at ABF and he had to move on. Garfield Weston's wife died, and he handed on the running of the family businesses to his two sons, Garry and Galen. Garry became chairman of ABF, while Galen went to run the Westons' Canadian operations.

Gulliver had had an understanding with Garfield that eventually ABF would float Fine Fare on the stock market in its own right. ABF would retain a controlling interest, but the move would enable Gulliver and other senior executives of the supermarket chain to have a direct stake. However, Garry dropped that plan. Gulliver said: 'I think he was right. I do not think I would want to float off subsidiaries of Argyll. It can take away from the strength of the group.'

Nonetheless, it marked the end of an important chapter in Gulliver's life, for he realised that he would now never be able to make his fortune at Fine Fare. He said of his seven years there: 'I learned a great deal during that period because I had to transform 25 separate food retailing businesses into a single coherent whole. This strenuous programme involved me and my management team in a very heavy workload. We worked long hours. The head office was open all day Saturday and all directors worked a full six-day week. It was this comprehensive grass roots experience as an operator which I contend has made me an effective independent businessman.'

But, for Gulliver, his role at Fine Fare lacked what he and probably most of his fellow company bosses would agree are the essential features of being an entrepreneur: the power to decide whether to raise significant blocks of capital and whether to make strategic takeovers or other major investments.

So at the end of 1972 he struck out on his own, but his independence proved short-lived. As part of his terms of leaving Fine Fare, the Westons imposed on him a restrictive covenant, which banned him from going into the area of his greatest expertise, food retailing, for eighteen months. But he was allowed to make food and wholesale it, so he bought into a public company called Oriel Foods and did just that.

It was the first time Gulliver had had to put his own money on the line, and at the time he found it an unnerving experience. 'I did not have any money,' he remembered. 'My 29 per cent stake in Oriel was costing me £1,250,000. I was able to raise £250,000 from my own resources, including stock options from Garfield Weston. I borrowed £1 million personally from William Brandts, the merchant bank. That was the biggest personal risk I had ever taken. I was very conscious of the interest – £100,000 to £120,000 a year – going out, or in fact added to my debt.'

Using the techniques he had learned at Fine Fare, he soon knocked Oriel into shape, buying a series of cash-and-carry wholesalers, keeping stocks low and cash high, and getting margins up. But after only two years RCA, the giant US television and radio corporation, made a takeover bid. They were offering a good price and Gulliver readily surrendered his independence.

'The idea was that Oriel would build a European food business for them. It attracted me because they were prepared to put very large funds behind us and give us major opportunities to build capital. The approach also came at a time when it was very clear that we as a country were getting into trouble. In 1974 the stock market went down in a straight line. We had two elections and a socialist government and things were looking pretty dodgy. Looking back, that was a very good decision of mine to take the RCA offer. We got 205p a share, which cleared my loans and made me a millionaire. It made no difference to me when I became a millionaire. I did not change my house or my car. I did not set myself financial goals like that, but I still had the desire to build a substantial food business.'

The partnership with RCA did not last long. The Americans changed their chairman and the new man wanted to return to what they knew best, electronics. In 1976 Gulliver tried something which was then almost unheard-of but has since become commonplace, a management buyout. It did not come off, mainly because the pound had taken one of its periodic dives against the dollar. This meant that RCA could not get back as many dollars as it had put in, without Gulliver having to pay an inflated amount of pounds.

So again he walked out. And again he suffered a restrictive covenant, as RCA was still running Oriel. This time he could not trade in the food business at all for another eighteen months. At the age of 45, James Gulliver was personally wealthy, but his career was at a crossroads.

He formed James Gulliver Associates as a private company to keep together what was already showing signs of being a winning team. While Gulliver awarded himself 75 per cent of the shares, the rest was divided between Alistair Grant, who first caught Gulliver's eye at Fine Fare, and David Webster, who had been at William Brandt, the merchant bank which had put together the financial package for Gulliver when he took over at Oriel. Both worked with him at Oriel. For two years Gulliver filled in time running a double glazing and bathroom showers company called Alpine Holdings. Meanwhile Grant and Webster, who were on the board of Alpine, were also moving into a small grocery wholesaling company in Shrewsbury, called Morgan Edwards. Grant and Webster were not tied by the RCA covenant, and so could go back into the food trade. They kept Morgan Edwards warm for Gulliver until he was free to take it over.

All the time he was kicking his heels Gulliver was plotting his return to the supermarket business. 'I wanted to build a big food multiple,' he explained, 'but, with the concentration of market share in the hands of a handful of major food retailers in Britain, I realised we would have to be bold enough to grow through acquisition, and quickly, if we were to reach a critical mass – the point where we were obtaining the economies of scale to enable us to grow organically. This meant having the support of the bankers and financial institutions of the City of London.'

So Gulliver did the rounds of the banking parlours. The price RCA had paid to take over Oriel had made him some influential friends in the financial community, and there was no shortage of others willing to hear his tale. There were sceptics at the time who doubted the wisdom of launching a supermarket chain in the teeth of an economic recession. But Gulliver argued cogently that there was no better time. He said: 'I believe, like Paul Getty, that the foundations of good businesses are laid in times of recession and therefore I, together with my top management team, had no hesitation in risking our personal resources and starting in food retailing again. There are some important advantages in operating in a recession. Both management and labour will more readily accept change. Very often lenders find it difficult to find people who want to borrow from them, and many potentially good businesses are put up for sale.'

In 1979, when Gulliver's restriction was over, James Gulliver Associates got together with two merchant banks, the London-based Charterhouse and Edinburgh's Noble Grossart, to pay £100,000 for twenty per cent of the shares in Louis C. Edwards, the Manchester butcher which was to be transformed into Argyll Group. Through his subsequent friendship with Louis Edwards, the deal also brought him a stake in Manchester United Football Club, where he duly became a director.

There followed a hectic series of deals designed to lift Edwards/ Argyll into the big league. Three months after stepping into the Edwards boardroom, he paid £1,800,000 for Yorkshire Biscuits. Towards the end of that year he picked up Furniss & Co., a biscuit maker, for £480,000. In 1980 there were four more takeovers: Cordon Bleu, the freezer centre group, in January for £2,650,000, the next month Dalgety Frozen Foods for £480,000, Morgan Edwards for £4,100,000 in March and seven months later Freezer Fare for £1,500,000.

That took the total value of the deals so far over £10,000,000 and set the stage for a satisfying triumph. Early in 1981 Argyll took over Oriel from RCA for £19,500,000. When Gulliver had bought his original shares in Oriel eight years previously, the company had been worth £4,300,000.

Gulliver's pace slowed a little, while he consolidated his mush-rooming empire. That autumn he made a bid for Linfood, the cash-and-carry group which was later renamed Dee Corporation, but at the point of victory the Government's Office of Fair Trading blocked the deal on the grounds that it was likely to cut down competition. In January 1982, Argyll acquired Pricerite, the supermarket chain, for £3,000,000.

Then Gulliver was ready to make the leap which would bring Argyll within reach of the likes of Sainsbury, Tesco and Asda. Although Argyll was valued on the stockmarket at only £45 million, Sir James Goldsmith asked Gulliver if he was interested in buying Allied Suppliers, the Liptons and Presto group. Argyll did so for £101 million.

'I knew quite a lot about Allied,' Gulliver explained modestly. 'It was a company I had watched from a distance.' In fact, he had pointed out its charms to Sir James Goldsmith, the Anglo-French food magnate, back in the late 1960s. Allied had had a long tradition as one of the established food retailing groups. It had been connected with Unilever at one time, and its shares had been reckoned important enough to be one of the constituents of the Financial Times index of thirty leading shares. In 1972 Sir James bought Allied to take his Cavenham Group into the big league. But ten years later he was intent on pulling his business interests out of Britain. So he sat down with Gulliver over a pot of coffee at the Ritz Hotel in London and they came to a deal. The easy way for Gulliver to pay for Allied would have been to give Goldsmith a huge block of Argyll shares. But that would have given Goldsmith control of the combined group, the last thing Gulliver wanted. And besides, Goldsmith wanted cash that he could take out of the country and reinvest in the United States.

A City merchant bank, Samuel Montagu, came up with a novel solution. They suggested floating on to the stock market enough Argyll shares to pay most of Goldsmith's £101 million, and borrow the rest. It sounds obvious, but it was unusual to go in for such a manoeuvre on such a large scale in the shares of a company which already had a share quote. Normally, Argyll shareholders would have been asked to take the extra shares through a rights issue. But the £80 million or so needed was too much to ask.

.There remained one more significant piece of tidying-up for Gulliver to do. Since 1979, in parallel with, but quite separately from, Argyll, he had been quietly developing a drinks production and distribution business, Amalgamated Distilled Products. He had realised from the start that if Argyll grew as he intended, it would sooner or later be stopped from making any more takeovers. Indeed, within three years, it had been prevented from pursuing Linfood and there had been murmurings that the Office of Fair Trading would have had its misgivings about the Allied deal, were it not for the fact that Goldsmith was apparently keen to sell. So eventually Argyll would need to find other outlets for its spare cash. A speciality distiller with a foothold in the US would fit as neatly as any. Amalgamated has three whisky distilleries, including a malt distillery in Gulliver's old home town of Campbeltown.

In 1983 he merged Amalgamated into Argyll. 'I decided to merge the two companies,' Gulliver explained, 'because it meant that I no longer had any conflict of interest about where my time would be best spent. But I also believe that as the major food retailers develop there will be no opportunity for acquisitions and we will be increasingly competitive, one with another. And as we are extremely strong cash generators in a restricted market, we shall have to diversify here or overseas. I think we should build a drinks business in the US, and go into food retailing there too.'

The keys to Gulliver's success have been a consistent vision of what he wanted and an enduring relationship with two close and trusted colleagues, Grant and Webster, in whom he could confide and bounce ideas off. Their skills complement one another. Grant has the retailing background, while Webster is the financial expert. Allied to Gulliver's strategic outlook, the three of them can very quickly pick a proposal to bits and see whether it can be put back together intact.

Gulliver described himself as 'a delegator, but with a tinge of ruthlessness'. He explained: 'A strong feature of our business is very strong financial control. We do very detailed profit plans for each operation with the executive concerned. If he fails to make that, and if it is due to his shortcomings, then perhaps the first failure would be acceptable – but the second would not.'

His method of delegation is to set limits, both in terms of money and men, below which he does not expect to interfere. Above those limits, though, he takes a direct hand. 'One thing I have had to do is train myself to be a delegator,' he admitted. 'At Fine Fare I inherited a poor management team and I felt initially that I would try and persevere with them, which placed a heavy burden on me personally to be involved at a much lower level than I should have. Following that I have had to get used to delegating. The tinge of ruthlessness comes through if things that are achievable are not achieved. But you have got to foster and encourage the best people. It's that extra effort that makes the difference. You need to know that someone will be working flat out, all hours if need be, to achieve the company's goals. Mind you, we are very much alive to the remuneration packages that are available nowadays. We have millions of share options out to our management.'

Gulliver immerses himself in reviewing and applying the group's annual plan. He reviews it with Grant, Webster and other key executive directors every month to make sure everything is on course. In 1984 the head office was moved from the outskirts of London to a small house in the backwater of Mayfair, so that Gulliver and a small team could think about and plan the long-term future of Argyll, free from day-to-day problems. Gulliver discusses all major policy changes with Grant, Webster and Colin Smith, the group financial controller, before putting them to the board, which meets every two months but can come together at any time if necessary. Below that level, executives have set limits on the amounts they can spend without referring the decision upwards for approval. Grant will vet the cost of new stores up to a further ceiling, beyond which it goes to Gulliver. 'The same goes for executive recruitment,' Gulliver said. 'Above a certain level, I make the choice. It's a hierarchical system. Of course there are disagreements from time to time at board level, but they do tend to be rare. We have strong communications at the top, and we do not tend to deal in surprises with one another.'

With a group of Argyll's present size, it is inevitable that Gulliver has to rely on his advisers even for the most important decisions. He explained: 'I suppose I would be regarded as a strong leader, but I try to avoid being regarded as autocratic. If we are spending, say, £7,000,000 on a new store, the marketing department will look at the catchment area and the likely turnover of such a store. There would be comments from the store's management, the development department who would have to build it and the accountancy department. Then it would come to me for approval, and after it had been through all those hands I would have to have a very strong conviction to turn it down. So it becomes a team effort.'

But Gulliver concedes that, even with such a thorough system, it is all too easy to make mistakes. 'There are always missed opportunities,' he said. 'For example, we could have been involved at an early stage with Bejam, the freezer centre group. In 1974 they were needing finance and we could have had a sizeable holding in Bejam for a few hundred thousand pounds.'

Meanwhile, Gulliver has been concentrating on developing and streamlining Argyll. His main effort in Britain is devoted to expanding the Presto supermarket chain. He is improving profit margins by closing unprofitable stores, opening about twenty new stores a year, selling more higher-margin fresh foods and selling more goods under Presto's own label. The drinks side is growing by buying and creating more brands to push through the system, both here and in the US.

Gulliver said: 'There is an old saying, that if you don't know where you are going, any road will take you there. Argyll knows where it is going and it will most assuredly get there. I would like to see us considerably larger. I would like us to be a much bigger food retailer. I do not see us being dominant, but sizeable. I see a significant proportion of our business, perhaps forty per cent, coming from the US. I see us going into areas we are not in at the moment. We regard ourselves as being in the business of selling any form of food and drink to the public, and that could take us into some very different markets from those we are in now. And I would like to see us get to a stock market capitalisation of £1 billion.'

By the end of 1985 his ambitions had soared well beyond that, as he launched an unsuccessful £2 billion bid for Distillers, the giant spirits group which makes Johnnie Walker, White Horse and Black and White whisky, Gordon's gin, Cossack vodka, Pimm's No. 1 and many other liquors. There is an undeniable tension within James Gulliver, as the Scots ethic of hard work and no nonsense wrestles with a restless urge to make up for lost time by acquiring lesser businesses which he knows he can improve upon. Perhaps the best thing the Weston family at Associated British Foods could have done was to hold Gulliver back from starting his own business, as he now acknowledges they inadvertently did. In so doing, they eventually released a bottled-up energy which shows no sign of being exhausted for some years to come. It is proving to be a very powerful fuel.

John Gunn

Why does anyone ever go into the City for a career? Being tied to a desk, juggling with figures all day, is not most people's idea of excitement. But to John Gunn and many of his contemporaries, juggling with figures is a dying art which still gives enormous satisfaction. 'It annoys me sometimes,' said Gunn, 'to see shop girls laboriously working the simplest sums out on bits of paper – 99 times two, that sort of thing.' As anyone brought up on a diet of mental arithmetic knows, you get the answer to that by taking two away from 200, leaving 198.

The ability to do infinitely harder sums than that at incredible speed can make or break fortunes in the foreign exchange and money markets. Gunn found he was quick as anyone at making those snap calculations and, when the time came, he found he also had a talent for running a business. The two together led him to create a fast-growing company called Exco International and make a fortune for himself. Then in September 1985 he suddenly walked out on the company he had done so much to create and set about starting a new career for himself in the City. 'I felt that the rest of the board didn't want to build the company up. I wanted to be more radical,' he explained.

Few people outside the City had heard of Exco, and even the name itself has a mysterious air about it. The group helps to oil the wheels of commerce by finding a home for spare cash. It acts as the broker to investors big and small, taking a commission for dealing in all sorts of securities from a unit trust nest-egg to stocks and shares, trade credits, loans, foreign exchange, gold and American real estate, operating through a worldwide network of offices.

The role of the go-between is growing by leaps and bounds in the financial world. Just as most home-buyers find they need the help of an estate agent, so more and more banks and investment houses find it is quicker and cheaper to turn to a broker to handle their dealings. Money brokers account for about half the world's transactions in that field, and the proportion is growing all the time. Above all, they offer their clients the enormous benefit of being anonymous: if a bank sells foreign exchange or loan notes direct to another bank, it may be giving clues about how it expects the market to move, and that can be valuable to a competitor.

As for Exco's anonymous-sounding name, that shows how self-effacing Gunn can be, and how unimportant he regards labels compared with what the people behind those labels actually do. When the company was being formed, they borrowed the name traditionally used by authors of accountancy textbooks. To illustrate a point such books usually invent an example based on a fictitious 'X Company'. Hence Exco. The group has, by chance, bought a 'Y Co', spelt WICO, and for good measure they have registered a 'Z Co', just in case it comes in handy.

If that sounds a trifle mickey-taking, not quite the image of the po-faced, bowler-hatted City gent, then it is not a bad reflection of John Gunn. It would be hard to imagine him in a bowler hat, let alone pin stripes. He is an iconoclast in the eyes of the City establishment, whom he in turn regards as letting Britain down by trying to hold on to their age-old privileges in the face of tough competition from the US and Japan.

The story of John Gunn's career begins with long walks around the Cheshire countryside with his maternal grandfather. 'He was very clever,' Gunn recalled. 'He started me off stamp collecting, for which I thank him, and he taught me a lot of the tricks of mental arithmetic. He would test me as we went on our walks.'

Gunn's father, the son of a blacksmith, was evidently no slouch at the numbers game either, and between them the two men kept young John up to the mark. Gunn senior became a butler at Arley, a big estate in Cheshire. There he met and married John's mother, a shop assistant. 'My dad did all sorts of things,' John said. 'He ended up on the goods side of London Midland Railways, but he had been a pro footballer in the Cheshire leagues, he could sing, he was very keen on reading, he played cricket up to good club standard well into his fifties. He was a bit of a dilettante, he never made the most of his talents. He was just an enjoyable guy to be with. It was my mother who instilled the Protestant work ethic into me.'

That work ethic took Gunn into a Church of England grammar school in Northwich and then on to Nottingham University. 'I wanted a university with good sports facilities, a good environment and small classes. I had been to London twice by then and I didn't like the size of it,' he said. He chose to read German at Nottingham, a decision which was to have a profound influence on his life.

'I didn't really know what I wanted to do,' he explained. 'German was a fairly practical choice. But what turned me on was the reflective aspects of it, particularly the literature in both the middle-high German and modern German periods. I still read more German literature than English.'

Inevitably his studies took him to Germany several times, culminating in more than a year spent teaching in Berlin. He went there in 1962, only a year after the Berlin Wall was first built, and quickly became caught up in the dramatic atmosphere of those days.

He was exposed to the sharp clash of East and West when tension and uncertainty were at their height. He attended Brecht's operas in East Berlin and played cricket for the British Military Intelligence team – known as the Optimists! – on the hockey field in the Berlin Olympic complex. The scorer for some of those cricket games was an East German refugee called Renate, who became John's wife. She had slipped over from East Berlin two days before the wall went up.

'That year in Berlin was the most formative year of my life,' Gunn said. 'It taught me two essential things. The first was that we in Britain are very lucky to be British and should work harder to protect that. The alternative is frightening. Secondly, the most important thing that had any bearing on my business was that it enabled me to spend time away from England, in another culture. When I returned from Germany, for the first few weeks I found it easier to speak German than English. I became that involved. So I do not take a particularly English view of the world around me. I am extremely patriotic, but not uncritically so. The experience has enabled me to build a business that is now no more than twenty per cent in this country. I do not really think it could have happened had it not been for such a formative experience.'

Gunn returned to England intending to embark on a PhD course, while Renate planned to take a degree in West Berlin. But that would have meant long separations for several years, so they decided to make a complete break, give up studying and settle in England. 'It sounds very noble, but you have to face reality,' said Gunn. 'Mind you, it had never crossed my mind before that I might have to work for a living!'

He headed off towards the world of finance for the same reason many young hopefuls go into the forces, because it offered the chance to see the world. Gunn explained: 'It struck me that the banks or the insurance companies could be interesting, as they might be able to let me make use of my ability to speak German. I didn't like the look of the insurance companies, because at that time they had the image of the man in his bicycle clips. So I went to Barclays Bank as a graduate trainee.'

Once there, he soon found himself working in the foreign branch in Manchester. 'It was extremely enjoyable,' he said. 'They pushed me through very quickly. I had a facility for foreign exchange because of my ability with mental arithmetic.' He also showed an early talent for reorganising, because he speeded up his operation so much that the other departments asked him to slow down. 'It was profitable business,' Gunn pointed out, 'so I went to the manager and told him I wasn't changing.'

This stand was hardly designed to increase Gunn's popularity with his colleagues, but Barclays obviously got the message that he was more than ready to move on. Soon afterwards there was a mass exodus of the bank's foreign exchange dealers in London, and Gunn was sent down as one of the replacements. There he might have stayed, had the German connection not reappeared to play a vital role in his career.

Gunn took up the story: 'At that stage Renate's father was very ill, and we had to spend quite a lot of money, both in visiting East Germany and sending medicines. We were financially very stretched. This was also a time when the foreign exchange markets were livening up, between 1966 and 1968, and people doing the same job as me elsewhere were earning twice or three times as much as me. I asked Barclays for more money. They said that they couldn't change the rules for one person, and if I got a rise they would have to put me on to a different scale from the other graduate trainees. Now it seems to me that loyalty is a two-way street, and there are limits on both sides.'

In that frame of mind, John set off for Germany to see his father-in-law for what turned out to be the last time. 'I was sitting in a train for 24 hours on that journey, and I had a lot of time to think,' he recalled. 'I felt that the bank was a very structured organisation, and maybe all banks were the same. They cannot seem to handle people who do not fit easily into their structure.' So he left to join Astley and Pearce, a money broking firm he had been introduced to by a close friend who was already working there. It was to prove to be another decision which had consequences on a scale he could not have imagined.

'There was a tremendous number of talented people there at that time,' said Gunn. 'I was broking foreign exchange. I was a pretty rotten spot broker, where you have to deal to get the best price in a currency at the going rate. But I was interested in arbitrage.' This is the considerably more complicated business of making money by seizing on the anomalies that crop up between different currencies and interest rates traded across different markets across the globe. A dealer might notice that the pound was trading at $1.26 in Frankfurt, while a dollar was fetching 255 Japanese yen in New York, but that a broker in Milan was willing to sell Dutch guilders for 70 yen apiece. Meanwhile, back in London the pound was changing hands for 4.3 guilders. If the eagle-eyed dealer could push a million pounds through that sequence while those rates held good, from Frankfurt to New York, to Milan and on to London, he would end up with £1,067,441, ignoring brokerage charges. It may not look very much, but a profit of £67,000 for possibly just a few minutes' work is what makes the City's wheels spin. And there are thousands of people scanning the screens run by Reuters and others, all searching for such opportunities. It makes 3-D chess look simple.

Such a competitive business demands a quick and agile mind to see the right move before anyone else. The broker who is half a second slow in getting his telephone order in can miss out completely. His clients, who are both banks and multinational corporations moving millions of pounds' worth of currency at a time, soon notice if one of their brokers is losing his touch. That is why it is a highly paid, high pressure, young man's game.

Once again, Gunn found new ways of operating. The Eurodollar market was growing fast. This is the market which developed during the 1960s in US dollars held outside the US. It gradually expanded to include any currency being traded outside its own borders, but it is still dollar-based.

Gunn said: 'I got people to let me have funds which they wanted to lend, to see if I could get a better deal by arbitraging. I was on the Swiss Franc desk, and I made that the dominant section in the firm.' Gunn was gratified to discover that Astley and Pearce was not too rigidly structured to deny him a pay rise and increased status.

The Bank of England presented Gunn with a heaven-sent opportunity to take off from there. It changed the rules in 1973 so that firms like Astley could deal directly with foreign banks in foreign exchange, instead of having to go through the British banks. Astley was one of the first to build a European network, in part because of Gunn's fluent German and his ability to work well with continental Europeans. It was a natural move to make him responsible for travelling round setting up the branches and, as time went on, returning to make sure the local managers had no problems and even covering for them on holiday.

Exhausting as it was for Gunn, the experience was invaluable because he was able to see the potential for developing new types of business, especially in the Far East. John had by this time got the taste for running a business, and was bristling with ideas if ever he got his chance.

He got that chance in 1975, when Astley's parent company, P. Murray-Jones Ltd, ran into big losses on commodity trading and was taken over by Gerrard and National, one of the City's leading discount houses. Gerrard was far-sighted enough to earmark 24 per cent of Astley's shares for the firm's new executive team as an incentive. Instead of dividing up these shares individually, the twelve top executives formed a separate company to hold them. That company was Exco.

Out of that twelve, Gunn was the one with the drive, bustle and energy to become managing director. He had suddenly emerged as an entrepreneur, through the natural development of his skills in the business and a strong view of where he felt the business ought to be going. 'I like to create an environment where people are not afraid to come up with ideas,' he explained. 'Nobody here is a money broker by background. We all read different things at university, so we have all got different casts of mind. It's like a senior common room: anyone with an idea can just walk through the door and talk about it. I am an enthusiast. I look at everything, even when I suspect it's a waste of time. You've got to be positive about it, because people appreciate that and bring you more ideas. You must never stop wanting to learn. My ego can easily be bruised, but that is not to say it should not be bruised. I put up ideas in debate, often when I expect them to be dismissed, to gauge the reaction. I act as a catalyst. But when I feel strongly about something I am 100 per cent a nuisance about it.'

Gunn contends that most City businesses are not difficult to run from the financial point of view. There is no money tied up in raw materials or stocks of finished goods. City rents are high, but there is normally a steady flow of income to pay for that. Despite sporadic efforts in recent years, there is very little trade union presence in the City, and what there is is still confined to the bigger targets, like the banks.

Said Gunn: 'The point at Exco was that we did not get involved in a big asset play. We did not have any trading activities in which we were taking positions. We were simply acting as intermediaries.' This in contrast to other firms, like investment banks, who make a lot of their money from asset plays, buying blocks of shares or loan notes for themselves, in the hope of selling at a profit. Exco misses out on those profits, but it also misses out on the risk and its clients know that Exco is not trying to compete with them.

What is needed are frequent, prompt and detailed reports on each part of the business. In that way the top management can quickly spot anything going off the rails, such as the commodity problems of Astley's former parent. That has cast something of a cloud over Gunn's approach to the business. because he is determined never to get into that sort of trouble again. He concedes that it makes him more conservative than he might otherwise be. 'I hate owing anyone anything,' he said. 'It's a great spur if you have to repay loans.'

It is noticeable that Exco prefers to raise money by issuing new shares than by borrowing. And nothing is done primarily for tax reasons. By running the business straightforwardly, Gunn and his co-directors were able to devote more energy to planning the future direction of the company.

It was a clever strategy to put the Astley executives' shares into a special company, for it bound their interests more closely together and they inevitably saw Astley as an extension of Exco, which duly became the master company. After tidying Astley and closing some of its less promising overseas branches, the Exco team's next move was to establish themselves in New York through a link with a money firm called Noonan.

But a major flaw was developing in the relationship with Gerrard and National. 'We were expanding fast and wanted more backing from Gerrard,' said Gunn, 'but it was never going to be worth it to them to divert significant amounts of money from their main business towards us.' So he found a way to escape from that straitjacket by replacing Gerrard with another backer.

'Most of the firms we went to wanted to have 75 per cent of Astley, leaving us with just the 25 per cent or so we had started with,' Gunn remembered. 'But we wanted a deal which would enable us to take over the whole of Astley eventually. We could have just walked out and started afresh, but that would have left Astley's 200 staff in the lurch.'

Through Roddy Macleod, a stockbroker, Gunn was introduced to Campbell Allan of Gartmore, one of the more go-ahead money management groups. 'He taught me a lesson that I have used ever since,' said Gunn. 'He simply asked me what we really wanted. It's a very good approach because it puts the other person at ease, makes you seem reasonable and you learn a lot more about the business you're talking about.'

Allan came up with a deal which enabled Gartmore to take Gerrard's stake in Astley, but on terms which would let control pass to Exco as and when they earned it. Several years later, Exco had done so well that it took control of Gartmore too! But that was after Gunn had done the most important deal of his life, in the Knickerbocker Café, in Greenwich Village, New York.

Gunn was beginning to look ahead to the time when he might be able to float Exco's shares on the Stock Exchange, to give the company a source of ready money for expansion. But he felt that money-broking on its own was not enough to put before the investing public. He wanted an extra activity, something different to fire the imagination, yet with a strong thread linking it back to the basic money business. Said Gunn: 'I decided that money-broking had got to the stage where it would not be able to grow at twenty or twenty-five per cent a year for much longer, but would settle down at ten or fifteen per cent growth. It was becoming a mature business.'

For some time Gunn had been fascinated by the prospects for high-speed information services. News agencies had existed since Reuters had started flying carrier pigeons across the English Channel during the last century. Things had speeded up since then, thanks to the telegraph and telephone, but it was Reuters which had taken the latest step forward. It had developed a system of transmitting and displaying financial information on a keypad-controlled monitor. This was instantly in demand wherever it could be installed.

'Reuters would not let brokers put their prices on to the system,' Gunn recalled. 'They wanted to develop it purely as an interbank system. We were rebuffed by them time and time again in our attempts to become a contributor. Yet it was a natural fit for us. I always believed that money-broking was really an information business. We were putting out hundreds of bits of information every day, and getting back the odd bit of commission.' So, as Reuters would not let him in, he decided to set himself up as a competitor.

There was only one other system within his reach, and that was Telerate, based in New York. This was one of those occasions when Gunn was prepared to be '100 per cent a nuisance', so determined was he to get it. In true cloak-and-dagger style, the final haggling over the price took place at a restaurant in Greenwich Village – the Knickerbocker Café. They struck a deal at

$75 million and Gunn took the next plane back to London. The money was raised in partnership with Guinnness Peat, the merchant banking and insurance group, but Exco subsequently bought them out.

'Information is the most used drug in the world,' Gunn explained. 'People are getting hooked on information, and it also gives dealers more confidence. Because Exco is a market animal we could suggest ideas or products which could influence the direction Telerate took. We could often see what the market needed. Telerate's people then got on with it, but they were extraordinarily good at reacting to the impulses from the market.'

The growth of Telerate has been remarkable. Within three years of Exco buying into it, it surged to the point where it accounted for just over half the group's profits and threatened to dwarf the traditional money-broking side. Customers pay for the information they receive. But if they contribute information as pure advertising, but do not receive any other information, then they pay nothing for their terminals. Telerate does not pay for the information it transmits.

But the competition in computer-based information is tough, and Gunn realised that it was going to get tougher. The survivors would have to work full time and flat out to be successful, and Exco could never devote that amount of money and effort to keep Telerate abreast of its rivals. In the summer of 1985 Exco sold it for £360 million.

The brush with Reuters taught Gunn an important lesson. 'If Reuters had let us become one of their customers we might never have ended up competing with them,' he pointed out. 'By not allowing us in, they concentrated our minds wonderfully on the question of how to overcome the problem.' Not that either of them is going to be treading on the other's toes for some time yet; the demand for financial information is growing too quickly for that. But the time may come when Reuters will regret having turned away such a determined opponent.

'I love to forgive, but I hate to forget,' said Gunn. 'I look in the mirror in the morning and count my blessings, but I also ask myself how to keep those blessings. I think that is just as important as jumping into the next new venture.'

Like several other entrepreneurs, Gunn is keen to play down the notion that he is moving too quickly for his own good. It was a doubt which during 1984 crept in among the stockbrokers who regularly debate whether the shares of Exco or its rivals are worth buying. Within six months up to March 1984, Exco asked its shareholders for £116 million to finance expansion through two hefty issues of new shares. At the time there were initial grumbles that it was too much, too quickly and betrayed a lack of planning.

Gunn, understandably, denied any such thing. 'The stock market was upset by that,' he admitted, 'but our major shareholders said they were perfectly happy. We were still a young company, and perhaps we had a longer horizon than the stock market itself. That money put our balance sheet in a very strong position to make the sort of moves we were going to have to make in the future, and less than a year after those share issues we noticed that our shareholders' register had been transformed. Every big fund you could think of was on it.' This was duly echoed by the stockbrokers' researchers, who by early 1985 were urging their clients to buy Exco shares.

Gunn used the extra money to expand into new areas. It bought into two London stockbroking firms, and paid £16 million for control of London Forfaiting, a trade finance business. 'We are entrepreneurial,' said Gunn, 'but we try and play it as safe as we can whilst being as bold as we can. I do not believe in the "not invented here" syndrome. It was our Zurich management which suggested we went into bullion broking. Leasing came from one of our directors who had been doing some work on tax shelters. You have got to have an incredibly open mind, because the possibilities can come from any direction. In the present rapidly changing environment, flexibility is one of the most important assets to possess.'

Gunn finds it hard to recall any major mistakes made by Exco in its short existence. Rather, he talks in terms of missed opportunities. 'The commodity losses at P. Murray-Jones Ltd slowed us down for several years,' he claimed, 'because we were determined the same thing would not happen to us, we were over-cautious. We took longer than we should have to get into the information business with Telerate, and we missed the last downcycle in the US for stock, bond and Government securities trading.'

Although Gunn had a strong team around him, it was clear that it was his personal stamp which characterised Exco's development into a rounded financial services group based on the principle of being the go-between for the growing number of players in the new numbers games that are springing up around the world. But as Exco's close rival, Mercantile House, has shown, there are many variations on this theme. So inevitably the course that any one company takes must be largely determined by the men at the top.

'I don't believe in the old pyramid structures for companies,' he said. 'People are too well-educated, too sophisticated for that any more. You have to treat people as adults if you expect them to respond as adults. That means giving them the freedom to grow. The people managing our branches in Tokyo, say, or Hong Kong, were running substantial businesses in their own right. We at board level had to expand our role so that we could leave enough room for others to come up.'

The result of that policy has been to create thirty millionaires within Exco. Naturally, as more join this happy club, their initial delight is replaced by the more durable qualities of a common interest in the survival and prosperity of the group, coupled with a mutual desire to preserve their fortune. Financial security, once achieved, is not lightly given up.

'I have never seen a place that is so self-critical,' Gunn disclosed. 'It is largely a question of ambition. You have to ask yourself, what do you want? Is it to make money? Is it to protect yourself? I have never been quite sure. It is a combination of what your shareholders are prepared to back and what they and the staff will be happy with. I am a "free-market socialist", in that I like lots of people to do well. The only way I can do that is to make sure the company makes a lot of money, so the staff makes a lot of money and the Exchequer makes a lot of money. I am as capitalistic as you can get, but I do not think the trappings are important. Creation of wealth is almost a duty, because of the widespread benefits that flow from it.'

Yet in the end John Gunn is acutely conscious of the need to stay apart, to reserve the right to make his own decisions. 'I am a loner, that has never bothered me,' he said. 'I'd rather observe and listen and think. As a kid I often felt I wanted to get away. I used to get on a bike and cycle to various places in north Wales and back, about eighty miles.'

It was that loner's instinct which led him to quit Exco without any clear plan for his own future. He was given a desk at British and Commonwealth Shipping, one of Exco's original backers, and he enjoyed himself wheeling and dealing on the stock market. But by 1986 he felt that his future would ultimately lie in starting up another financial services company. 'I don't know where I will be, long-term,' he said, 'but I do know that I want to be in the financial sector. It's exciting and there is a lot happening. I like making decisions, it comes easily to me, and I want to be in a position where I can be the one setting out the strategy.'

Instead of cycling to north Wales, Gunn relaxes these days with skiing or walking holidays. In between times he is a director of the English Chamber Orchestra, and plays golf and cricket. But he can now claim to have outlived the despairing warning from his head-master in his last school report: 'Life, alas, is not a game of cricket.'

Noel Lister

When MFI Furniture Group received a takeover bid in April 1985, eyebrows were raised at the fact that Noel Lister, the co-founder of the business, had sold his personal shareholding for £40 million in cash before the ink was dry on the deal. But then not many people outside the company knew that he was building a 103-foot racing yacht to take him round the world.

While the outgoing, larger-than-life character of MFI's chairman, Derek Hunt, had been capturing the column inches, the company was very much the creation of the spare, self-effacing Lister and his late partner, Donald Searle. Although it is not unknown for some of the most successful entrepreneurs to shun publicity, to a spectacularly, obsessive degree in one or two cases, there are few who limit their own role in their master company to the barest essentials in quite the way that Lister did.

Yet he retained the title of chief executive until the moment he sold and he made sure those bare essentials counted, in terms of the direction of the business and the bottom line of profits. Now he can reckon himself one of the few entrepreneurs to have cashed in his chips in time to enjoy life without a care in the world – and more money than a roomful of pools winners could dream of collecting.

MFI began life as Mullard Furniture Industries, Mullard being the maiden name of Searle's wife, Joan. It now ranks as Britain's biggest furniture retailer, with its black and red warehouses on the outskirts of towns and cities from Aberdeen to Plymouth. While Sir Terence Conran revolutionised furniture retailing through his insistence on a strong design theme, MFI sold aggressively on price. But, as both firms moved into their third decade, they came closer together in outlook. Sir Terence's Habitat is more price conscious, while MFI is gradually introducing more design flair.

Yet for Noel Lister it all started with the simple realisation that he loved to trade. And he began his trading career in the army, in a strictly unofficial capacity. Aged eleven when the Second World War broke out, Lister was called up towards the end of the war. He remembered: 'The first time I realised that there was a profit to be made was when the weekly cigarette ration came round every Friday. I didn't smoke, but if I held on to my cigarettes until the following Thursday, when demand was high, I could sell each one for two cigarettes from people's ration the next day. We were given fifty cigarettes a week, so after a week I had 100, and then 200 and so on. That's how I realised there was a profit to be made from what you might call wheeling and dealing.'

While squeezing his mates' tobacco ration might not have been the best way to win the popularity polls, Lister's next money-making plan was more calculated to endear him, at a price. During the war he was sent to the Middle East, like thousands of others, in a troop ship. Because of the lack of space, there was little for the soldiers to do during the voyage except lie on their hammocks.

Lister takes up the story: 'I realised that I could get a milk churn full of tea from the galley for a price which meant I could fill a mess tin at a cost of a penny. But I could sell a mess tin of tea to the others in their hammocks for twopence. I used to make £4 a day doing that, on a trip which used to last ten days – and this was forty years ago! I came back three times from the Middle East during the war, and did the same thing each time.'

That firmly decided Lister on a peacetime career as a trader. The London of the immediate postwar period was bristling with opportunities for someone with his instincts. Wartime inflation, combined with the end of the awful uncertainties that went with the constant threat of attack, meant that people had spare cash in their pockets but nothing to spend it on. Everything could be bought – or sold – for a price if you knew the right person.

But before he could dive into this swirling pool of goods and cash, Lister had to learn the ropes. First of all he went to work at Bowmans, a furniture shop in Camden Town, north London, where he found himself in the second-hand department. A feature of this department was that, unlike other parts of the store, members of the public would come in to offer things for sale.

'Sometimes old ladies would come in and throw their hands up in despair,' he said with a smile, 'because they had a whole roomful of furniture and carpets they wanted to get rid of. So I used to say, "let me come round and I'll clear the lot for you", and I used to sell it on the side. Eventually Bowmans warned me about not working for myself, but by this time I realised that I had a natural inclination to buy and sell.'

So he left Bowmans and set up on his own in 1951 with just £17. He did not need any more than that to start with, because he had no premises and no staff. There was just himself, buying some of this and selling some of that, taking a living out of what was left over. One of his early coups was to buy some fire-damaged woolly toys, which he shampooed and sold round the shops.

From there, he joined the small army of traders who dealt in Government surplus stock in the 1950s. Huge jumble sales of goods were auctioned off, and one or two people started chains of shops specialising exclusively in the taxpayers' cast-offs. 'There was a period of four or five years when I had a hell of an education doing this,' said Lister. 'You'd have to deal in anything that came along – duffle coats, searchlights, demob suits, a quarter of a million shaving brushes, on one occasion sixty fire engines which we sold to the Middle East.'

Gradually he built up enough spare cash to open a shop of his own, and he went into partnership with someone he had met in the Government surplus trade, Donald Searle. That was the genesis of MFI, harnessing Lister's trading skills to Searle's ability to handle people. Searle had been selling his Government surplus stock through mail order, and Lister persuaded him to use this technique on Lister's old stamping ground, furniture. 'One day I had a new chair and table which were worth advertising. We sold 500 sets, twice what we expected. That was really the start of the business.'

Mullard Furniture Industries was incorporated in 1964, the same year that Habitat started. That was not entirely coincidental, for both firms in their different ways were responding to rapidly changing public tastes, in terms of the furniture being offered and the way in which it was sold.

Lister and Searle expanded their mail order business to the point where it was making profits of nearly £1 million a year. But the problems of rail and road transport forced them to change their approach in two radical stages. 'We were sending out huge quantities of furniture by this time,' said Lister, 'but a high percentage was becoming damaged. So we said, let's send it to the customer for him to assemble – and that was the beginning of flat-pack furniture. Then we got into further difficulties when British Rail and British Road Services cut their staff to one per load. Instead of the packages being handed from one loader to another, they tended to be chucked about by the one man. Again the damage rate went up, so we had to stop mail order altogether.'

By that forced route, MFI found itself in the business of selling flat-pack furniture from warehouses, now the accepted system for retailing low-priced household goods. The firm had six shops already, and it started opening one a month. And they discovered that they were able to cut prices so drastically that the customers were willing to travel miles to get to these new-style stores. Lister claims that this enabled MFI to become the first retailer in Britain to embark on the out-of-town idea, making use of the low rents on the suburban fringes.

'The byword at the time was, if you can produce an article at half the normal high-street price then you could draw the customer to any part of the country,' said Lister. 'We did it, and still do it, by offering the manufacturers big orders which enable them to plan long production runs on the most modern machinery. I remember seeing a folding bed in Gamages, in Holborn, for £20. I wanted to sell it for £9.95, so I went to the manufacturer and asked him how many we would have to order for him to be able to sell to us for £7. He said 10,000, and we sold them within a month.'

By 1970 MFI was pushing on towards a chain of fifty shops, and Lister admits it was becoming something of a grind. The formula had been established, and it seemed to be just a question of repeating it round the country. But then a personal tragedy intervened, with profound consequences for the company.

Because he was feeling stale, Lister set off on a trip round the world with his wife and two friends. He loves sailing, and they took a yacht down to the Canaries, across to the Caribbean, through the Panama Canal and on to Tahiti. The idea was that he would go off for three months, moor the boat, return to work for three months and then set off again. But when they got to Tahiti, they were told that Donald Searle had been killed in a gliding accident. They sold the yacht there and then, and flew back to London.

The loss, both personal and professional, was a mighty blow. It made Lister rethink his outlook. As he put it: 'Donald was a first-class manager and entrepreneur and his emphasis was on people, he was so good with people and that was my weakness. I have never been good with people; I have always been good with things. But during my three months away, other people in the company had been growing. I came back and I couldn't recognise some of them because they had had to make their own decisions while I was away. I learned a very valuable lesson, that you have to delegate. So often entrepreneurs resist this and cling on to every decision themselves, when what most of them are good at is wheeling and dealing. That's what I loved: the next deal.'

In his last couple of years at MFI Lister was spending up to a third of his time sailing, and working 'bloody hard' in the company during the rest of the year. He delegated everything except what he knew he was good at: the trading side of the business, advertising and marketing. Property dealing was handled by one subsidiary and the management of the stores by another. Lister was on the board of neither.

'The idea of a separate subsidiary for the furniture centres was introduced by Jack Seabright, who was joint managing director until a few years ago,' said Lister. 'He wanted to set up a board to make the day-to-day decisions without the founding entrepreneur poking his nose in everywhere. It was a clever move. If I'd been in there, I'd have been hassling all the time, arguing the toss. They didn't normally make decisions that affected me, and if they did, well, I was represented. When we had a store refit, I was in there saying we have got to have wallpaper in all the bedrooms and that sort of thing, but the day a board has a committee to decide a price you start going downhill, because the decisions will not be made quickly enough.'

Sunday trading was a good example of Lister exercising his right to take part in the internal debate, without taking a public stance on the issue. At MFI's north London headquarters it did not take a formal board meeting to exchange views; the people involved simply met in Lister's own comfortable and spacious office. 'We never had a vote in the company on the main board, and that might have been something to do with it,' Lister added.

When Searle died, much of the added responsibility was taken off Lister's shoulders by Arthur Southon, who joined MFI as an accountant and became chairman. Lister recalled: 'After Don's death Arthur became a close friend and very much a confidant I could bounce ideas off. There were so many things I wanted to do, but Arthur would caution me if I was in danger of getting too many balls in the air at the same time.'

More recently, the lynchpin has been Derek Hunt, the burly extrovert who worked his way up through the company and took over as chairman from Southon in 1984. He was the face of MFI to the outside world, including the important job of talking to the City's bankers, brokers and investment managers.

'I used to go round our new stores when they were opened,' Lister explained, 'but I generally visited the competition far more than our own stores. I tended to concentrate on the trading side of the business. The people I saw on a regular basis were our advertising director and his right-hand man, our advertising agency's account director, our buying director, marketing director and our joint assistant managing director, John O'Connell, who handled merchandise and distribution. And I saw every buyer and assistant buyer every week.'

Lister admitted modelling his business on the best elements of three other companies: McDonalds, the American hamburger restaurant chain, the Swedish-based IKEA furniture retailer, and Marks and Spencer. McDonalds was selected for the management's meticulous attention to detail. 'In America, they even tell the staff how to put a dustbin lid on a dustbin,' Lister said admiringly, 'and I believe that if you want well-managed stores, you have to give detailed instructions on what you want done.'

IKEA is little known in Britain, but several leading retailers over here have paid homage to its brilliant approach to marketing. Lister felt the comparison particularly acutely, because IKEA started at about the same time as MFI and its founders have a very similar background. 'They would sell just like a grocer,' said

Lister, 'pricing goods at cost or less to get the customers into the stores.'

Although MFI may not have gone that far, it borrowed the IKEA theme of banging the drum in a big way to pull in the public. And it was IKEA that pioneered the policy of building stores on greenfield sites, in some cases as much as fifteen miles out of town. The Swedes would duly pile into their Volvos and drive out there, for the sake of the lower prices. But to that formula IKEA has added a more adventurous dash of design to the products. Lister was more cautious. 'Once we'd got customers coming to our stores in large numbers we began to educate them to more design-conscious furniture,' he said, 'but we were followers rather than leaders in this respect – at half the price. If we thought our customers might be interested in a certain type of table, we had to be sure we were going to sell thousands of them.' The inescapable point being that thousands of Swedes are more likely to take a chance on a differently designed piece of furniture than the equivalent number of British consumers. That is something that British retailers and their suppliers have had to put up with from one end of the shopping precinct to the other.

But undoubtedly the strongest corporate influence on Lister was Marks and Spencer, in two principal areas: keeping up staff morale and relations with manufacturers. Apart from the now-common extras, such as sports centres and health insurance, paying greater attention to staff welfare and standards of dress was part of Lister's awakening to the need for a loyal and happy workforce. 'If you want the staff 100 per cent behind you, you've got to be 100 per cent behind them,' was one of his mottoes.

The second debt to Marks and Spencer, the development of a close relationship with suppliers, was central to Lister's business philosophy. M & S transformed the way in which manufacturers and the leading retailers dealt with one another. Under the traditional, hit-or-miss set-up, a factory would produce samples of a new line and take them round the shops' buyers. If they liked it, and it fitted in with their overall image, a price would be struck for a given size of order. But what Marks and Spencer wanted from their clothes suppliers when they embarked on this strategy was greater reliability and uniformity. They also wanted greater control over the prices they charged, and they realised that the only way to achieve that was to play a far greater part in the planning stage. That meant design, costings and, in the end, every part of a supplier's conduct of his business – right down to insisting in some cases that they install canteens.

For MFI, it was a logical consequence of building business by aggressive price-cutting. Manufacturers could see that this was a way to boost their production dramatically, and that put the two sides in the bargaining, the shopkeeper and the supplier, suddenly on the same side of the table for a large section of the negotiations. Before M & S, no one had been able to order enough to be that important to a producer. For some years now, they have recognised that it is in their interests to open their books and in some cases their deepest trade secrets to a retailer who can show that he can deliver the extra work.

'If it's fair for someone to make a five per cent profit margin on his contract,' said Lister, 'then it was fair for us to look at his detailed costings and compare them with those of other manufacturers. And if he puts that profit to buying new and better machinery, then it benefits us in the long run.' In the case of a bed, that meant finding out how much the cloth costs, the springs, the screws and the cover cap for the screw. Only in that way could both sides agree on exactly what is necessary within a given price bracket. Lister would sometimes go back down the production process one step further, and take part in the talks with his suppliers' suppliers.

Lister explained: 'The information is never made secret from one manufacturer to another. They are exchanging new ideas all the time, and this cross-fertilisation has helped our manufacturers because if one of them has a brilliant idea they can all benefit. During my early years I learned that there were two sides to every deal, and it had to be seen to be fair to both sides. There is no future in it otherwise. There are not enough mugs, and even the mugs won't come back a second time if they feel they've had a bad deal. Both sides have got to be happy, and you have got to be able to look from both sides of the fence. As soon as we started to sell new furniture, as opposed to second-hand, we got very close to our manufacturers and told them exactly what we wanted and the price we were willing to pay. We changed only two manufacturers in twenty years, although we added a few over the years.'

Lister does not admit to having made any big mistakes in his business career, but cheerfully owns up to 'thousands of small ones'. He said: 'As long as you are prepared to put your hand up to a small mistake, you don't make big ones. If a new idea wasn't making a profit in two weeks I would put my hand up, and I expected my managers to do the same. One of the most important things was that you had to be making decisions constantly, and you could only do that so long as you recognised the mistakes and stopped them quickly enough.'

MFI's trading record is a vivid testimony to Lister's ability to nip mistakes in the bud. Between the beginning of June 1974 and the end of May 1984, turnover rose from £15.2 million to £302 million and profit before tax went from £78,000 to £39.1 million. This performance was helped by one or two takeovers, notably the Status Discount chain, but it broadly reflected solid, well-managed growth in a market which hardly existed in its present form before MFI came along. As the group expanded, the group's shares became more widely spread. By 1985 there were nearly 6,000 shareholders, and Lister personally had an eight per cent stake.

'We had stores all over the country, and it was really a matter of improving the design, quality and service to our customers, and expanding the range,' said Lister. The stores were being upgraded from units of 25,000 square feet to 50,000 square feet and new lines were being added all the time. In 1985 the big push was into carpets, and Lister was also creating a springboard for a much wider campaign to become recognised as a provider of virtually every household need.

He invited do-it-yourself and electrical retailers to join MFI in combined edge-of-town centres. Someone who turns up to buy a bed, say, may be tempted next door to buy a bedside lamp or a tin of paint. An obvious next step after that would be for MFI to take over more of these extra lines itself.

However, Lister was too cautious to plunge in head first. 'I feel it's so important to get what you are doing right,' he said. 'We never diversified; we tended to concentrate on what we knew. I could not go into a business I did not understand myself.'

Lister was especially chary of getting into electrical goods. He moved into the basic kitchen equipment such as cookers, washing machines and fridges, but did not relish taking on the likes of Dixons in the television, hi-fi and gadget end of the market. This is in contrast to his friend, Sir Philip Harris of Harris Queensway, who tried to take over the Comet electrical chain but was outbid by Woolworths.

'I couldn't have run my business in the way Phil does,' Lister admitted, 'and some of my people could not understand how I was so pally with him. But you need competition, and I enjoyed the banter and geeing ourselves up that goes on with another competitive entrepreneur.'

Mild as Lister seems at first blush, he is an intensely competitive person. He admits that he loves competing, likes winning even better, and hates losing – whether the contest is a game of cards or a major business deal. Nowadays, he unleashes his competitiveness on the challenging sport of ocean yacht racing and in 1984 won the Yacht of the Year award, the top trophy for the sport in Britain. But this streak goes back a long way. Lister recalled how he and Donald Searle used to have a weekly squash match for a small cup they had had engraved. On one side was written: 'I, Donald, admit you, Noel, to be my superior at squash', while the other side said: 'I, Noel, admit you, Donald, to be my superior at squash'. As a result of this long series of 'friendly' games they each had a spell in hospital. 'Anybody who is not competitive, to my mind, loses a lot out of life,' said Lister.

So strongly did he feel about the need for this spirit to run through MFI that he built competition into every conceivable part of the business. This was enshrined in a company-wide bonus system, running from the salesmen through to incentives for each store, warehouses and even head office, as well as an executive share option scheme. Lister was also very keen on keeping the staff up to the mark by encouraging competition within the company for the best or most improved store, or the best-kept warehouse. The reward could involve taking a planeload of prize-winners for a long weekend to a spot in the sun, like Tangiers.

Lister's own get-away-from-it-all ambitions are considerably broader than Tangiers. 'I've been building a boat and I want to go round the world and finish the trip I never completed when Don died,' he said. 'I want to go to Indonesia, and I'd like to explore the ice floes of Vancouver – something you can really only do in a boat.' His new craft was being launched in 1986, and he is planning to take in the Great Barrier Reef and then sail round to Perth, at the other end of Australia, to see the next Americas Cup race.

But Lister also has ideas for helping young people who have not had his breaks. 'I'd like to get involved with different forms of outward bound operations, like the Operation Drake expeditions,' he said. 'You can take a bunch of underprivileged lads with chips on their shoulder, but once they've crossed an ocean together, they're ten feet tall.'

Lister keeps himself younger than his 58 years by swimming twenty lengths a day, windsurfing – and surrounding himself with younger people. At the time he sold out, most of his main board were aged between 35 and 45, despite the fact that in the main they had been with the company for ten or twenty years. The senior executives were mostly home grown, which means that the company rarely made any mistakes about promoting people into the wrong job. 'I still enjoyed the business,' said Lister, 'but towards the end I tired more easily than I had used to. I encouraged younger people to come forward so that there was plenty of steam in the business. I used to look forward to coming in on a Monday morning, I was all geed up, and I expected everyone else to be the same. As long as you get a kick out of the business it's great, but once you start not to get a kick – and I began to feel that – you're as well to get out and leave it to a younger team.'

His advice to anyone starting their own business is to pick a specialist area, concentrate on it and do not be distracted by the fact that someone else may be making more money. 'It's so easy to get distracted,' he said, 'but you must improve your own business. And of course, it's hard work. You have got to be prepared to put the hours in – and enjoy it. In business, if you are persistent you normally arrive. It's the old tortoise and hare story. You don't have to be super good, someone who is super good usually starts to ease off. That's so easy to do. Money is not that important: it's the competitive edge that's most important. That is what has driven me.'

Under the pressure of that competition, Noel Lister identified and to some extent anticipated a considerable change in British social habits. Until 1950 or so, furniture was bought and sold with the reverence due to future family heirlooms. The lighter, even spindly, furniture which appeared during the 1950s helped to dispel that attitude. But the missing link ushered in with the more easy-going 1960s was a more streamlined approach to retailing. While Habitat was piling its earthenware pots to the ceiling, MFI was turning tables, chairs and cupboards into so many screw 'n' glue assembly kits. The two chains cater for very different audiences, but each has changed the lives of millions of people for the better. And that transformation has some way to go yet.

Stephen Marks

To the outsider, the fashion business is notorious for the speed at which fortunes can be made and lost. Yet a surprising number of the top designers seem to have had a remarkable amount of staying power: Coco Chanel, Yves St Laurent, Pierre Cardin, Hardy Amies, Laura Ashley, Mary Quant. While the durability of that glittering group is beyond question, a new generation is beginning to push up behind them for a place in the gallery.

Among them is Stephen Marks, who floated his French Connection Group on the stock market in 1983 when he was 37 and within a year saw the value of his shareholding in the company soar to more than £40 million. If that looks suspiciously like an overnight success, bear in mind that he started backing his own flair for design by striking out on his own as far back as 1969, when Quant was already 35 and an established name.

Marks is a bearded, burly guy who has always preferred to do things his own way. He resents some of the chores of success, which for him include trying to persuade the dark-suited ranks of the City's stockbrokers and fund managers that he really is running a serious business, and never mind the stylish but casual clothes he likes to wear. 'They think we're just a bunch of people wobbling around,' he said, 'but we're not. We work bloody hard.'

From a modest launch pad turning out women's coats and suits under his own name, he has put together a group which spans the world, designing for the French Connection label in London, making up clothes in Turkey, India and Hong Kong and selling them in Paris, New York, Los Angeles and Tokyo as well as in the UK. There are French Connection shops in Kingston-upon-Thames and Cambridge, Glasgow and Guildford, Manchester and

Manhattan, and a growing number of other affluent towns and cities.

Yet it could have been very different. When Stephen Marks left the local secondary modern school in Harrow, north London, his first thought was to see if he could become a world-class tennis player. 'I spent the first six months after I left school playing tennis,' he recalled. 'I was pretty good, I played for my county and at Junior Wimbledon. This was in 1963, when there were no professionals at Wimbledon. I thought I might make it, but I realised I couldn't. I lived by doing odd jobs, and my father helped me along, even though he didn't think it was a good idea. I might have made it if I'd worked at it. But I didn't have the dedication. It just wasn't in me.'

Marks' father owned a hairdresser's in Harrow, so it was not long before the pressure grew for seventeen-year-old Stephen to relegate tennis to a hobby. He admitted: 'I had to find a job. My pocket decided that. I had always got on with people, talking to people was of importance to me. I went for a job with one of the big chains of women's clothes shops. One of the people doing the interviewing knew my father. He was in the women's coat business, and asked me to work for him. I didn't like the look of the big chain, and I really didn't have too much of a thought in my head at that time, so I just drifted in to this fellow's coat business. I worked there for six years. I made the tea, swept the floors, delivered the coats – you name it. It was great training, although it was purgatory at the time.'

Marks was to go through just one more employer before he set up on his own. Both had their faults, but as Marks readily admits, both taught him tricks of the fashion trade which he tucked away for future use.

He explained: 'I really have to thank Sheraton, my first employer, because it was one of the first companies in the country to have a computer, back in 1964, and they showed me what a really well-run firm could be like. Everything they did was excellent as far as administrative controls were concerned. But they forgot that you have got to have a product. That put the nail in the coffin for them, eventually.'

On Saturday mornings Sheraton had what they called range review meetings, when the staff would be shown the latest models which they would have to start selling the following week. 'The designer used to die a death every time,' said Marks. 'The sales people said they couldn't sell the style, and the production people kept saying the design couldn't be made up, and why couldn't we take this or this off to make it easier. In the end all the clothes used to look the same. I was about eighteen then, and I would sit at the back and listen to all this. One time they asked me what I thought, so I said that I thought they all looked the same and they said shut up, what do you know, so I shut up, what do I know? But it made me realise that clothes have to be designed well and have to look different if they are going to sell.'

Fashion being, like beauty, very much in the eye of the beholder, needs to be sold, and the lot of the rag trade firm's travelling rep is often a thankless one. But for the young Marks the days of driving rain and cancelled orders were eclipsed by balmy sunshine and high adventure.

'I used to have a great time on the road,' he recalled. 'Once I had to sleep in the back of the van because I couldn't get a hotel room for the night. There was a lot of freedom, though. North London was part of my territory, and all the young salesmen used to go to Kingsbury swimming pool on Wednesday afternoons because that was half-day closing in the area.'

But that was after he had got into the swing of things. Getting started was not so easy. He said: 'On my first day selling they gave me an area with no customers, so I couldn't do much damage. I was so nervous. I decided on a strategy: I would put a coat over my arm and walk in the shop with it like that. It wasn't a bad idea, but it didn't stop me getting thrown out of all sorts of places. The first few weeks were very harrowing. One time I had a new line, a dress and matching coat. I went into this shop, where the buyer was a middle-aged lady who had been in the business all her life. I showed her this new line, and she immediately said "What does your firm know about making dresses? You only do coats, don't you?" I was just assuring her that we had that completely under control, and I was just unzipping the dress to show her – when the zipper came off in my hand! I died, but she just said perhaps I could come back when we'd learned to put in zips properly.'

But after a while Marks began to learn some of the dodges that the managers of ladies' dress shops would get up to in their efforts to avoid salesmen. 'There was another fellow in Watford, who I was told only came in on Fridays,' he recalled with a grin. 'So every Friday I would call on him, and every Friday he wouldn't be there. This went on for a year, before one of the girls in the shop took pity on me and told me that what was happening was that whenever this man saw me coming he would go out the back and along the alleyway to another shop he owned four doors down the street. So I knew what I had to do: I had to park my van outside the first shop as usual, and then dash up the alley and catch him just as he was going out the back. That's exactly what I did. I confronted him with a coat over my arm, and he just broke up laughing! Incidents like that certainly taught me not to be afraid of anything in business.'

Marks was eventually made assistant sales director at Sheraton, and after two years he was approached by the firm that had the UK licence for Louis Feraud, the French high fashion designer of women's suits, with the idea of launching a coat range for young women under the name Miss Feraud. Marks did not know it, but he was in for another eye-opener.

He said: 'On my first day there, they showed me round. The showroom was immaculate. It was fitted out in the latest style and looked a picture. Then they opened the door to the workroom, and it was like being back in the Stone Age: dingy, overcrowded and completely disorganised. In the end I had to do everything myself, from running the sales side and production to stock control. They were making wonderful clothes, probably the most expensive clothes in England at that time, and they were using wire hangers for them and switching them on to wooden hangers when they were being delivered! I spent two years travelling the country selling Miss Feraud. The company got off to a cracking start. I was doing fourteen hours a day, six days a week. I was loving it, because for me it was my own business. I was doing everything and I knew what was going on.'

By that stage Marks had met the first of three men who were to change the course of his career. He was a fellow tennis fanatic called Peter Collins, who when Marks met him was already running his own successful dress company, known as Selection at Peter Collins. They became close friends, and Marks regarded Collins as his mentor.

Marks said of his hero: 'He asked me to leave the Louis Feraud firm to work for him, but I didn't think I would feel comfortable partly because we were friends, and because I hadn't worked with dresses before. I'd only worked in coats and suits up to then, which are quite different. They're tailored garments, they have to have padding and shape put into them. Dresses don't need that sort of thing, and it's a completely different approach – like being a journalist on *The Sun* instead of *The Times*.'

So instead, Collins suggested to Marks that as he was doing so much for his new employers he would be better off starting his own business and working for himself rather than working for somebody else. Again Marks demurred. 'I was happy and I was learning, so I didn't mind,' he explained.

But he was becoming increasingly conscious that he was working very hard for not very much in return. So he brought matters to a head. 'I said to the people running the firm, I'm doing half a dozen people's jobs and not getting paid enough for one. So they said you can be a director. I asked them, does that mean I get shares in the company? No, they told me. Does it mean I get more money? No. So I said in that case I do not want to be a director. They obviously didn't understand me, so I thought why not go out on my own? Two years from the day I joined I gave my notice in. And do you know, they made me work out my notice for three months. It was torture. But I decided I would work as hard as ever, just to show them. Then I went off in the evenings to try and get my own business started.'

Marks began, naturally enough, by designing and producing the sorts of clothes he was most familiar with up to that time, ladies' coats and suits. The youth cult of the swinging sixties was in full flow, and he aimed himself head-on at the young affluent market. He was also brash and self-confident enough to follow the then trend of personalising the names of fashion firms. He simply stitched 'Stephen Marks' into the clothes he sold. 'After my experience at Sheraton, I started with the idea that production was the most important thing,' Marks said. 'If it doesn't sell at retail, you ain't in business. You have got to have organisation, and you have got to deliver on time. It's no good being even a little bit late, because the mood can change and the retailer can miss those sales for ever: he's on to the next look.'

The Stephen Marks label soon became associated with smart and elegant suits at a price high enough to be affordable only by a fashionable minority. That meant that he could build in a healthy profit margin, but volume was automatically restricted. Marks recalled: 'For the first six months I did not draw a penny from the business. My flatmate even helped to pay the rent on the flat we shared. In the first year we had £180,000 turnover and made £18,000 profit. But that first year seemed like ten years. I had borrowed £7,000 from the bank and £10,000 from Peter Collins to get started. But every month that I was owing money to the bank and to my best friend just made me depressed.'

In the second year Marks doubled his profits to £36,000, enabling him to pay off his friend's loan. Marks offered Collins the chance to stay in the company as a shareholder, an offer which neither of them realised at the time would eventually have been worth millions. But he declined because he wanted Marks to have the satisfaction of succeeding on his own merits, without any doubt about where the credit lay. It was a selfless act which still leaves Marks shaking his head in admiration today.

Not long afterwards, Marks was to meet someone else who would have a fateful effect on his business. This was a Paris designer called Pierre D'Alby, who was the original French Connection although he never himself became part of Marks' company. 'Once the business got going,' Marks explained, 'I felt I needed a collection, instead of just making one-off garments. So I went to Paris and met all the fashion companies over there. That's where the name of our company came from. At first it was going to be French Collection, but then one day I was sitting in a car behind the London Palladium theatre with a friend who suddenly suggested calling it French Connection instead, after the film which had recently come out.'

In the early days, the connection took the form of Marks selling D'Alby's clothes in London. But it was to assume a much more far-reaching form when D'Alby came back from a trip to Hong Kong with a quarter of a million shirts. D'Alby had been bowled over by the incredibly low price, but 250,000 was far more than he could handle, so Marks took some off him and thought no more about it. But D'Alby had different ideas. Said Marks: 'Because I spoke English, which is more widely known in Hong Kong than French, he wanted me to go out there and fix up suppliers for him. I wasn't keen and didn't see much future in it, but in the end he said he would pay for me to go. So why not? I'd never been out there before. This was in 1972. On the way I stopped off in India and found there were also plenty of people who could be persuaded to make up dresses at low cost. I remember the first consignment we had: it was tightly bound in hessian, and when I cut it open it just exploded with clothes as they escaped from the packing! Of course, they were badly creased, but we gradually got things the way we wanted them. One year I was in India fourteen times. I used to go south to buy fabric, then come back north to get it made up.'

To take advantage of the high volume and low costs the Indians could offer, Marks had to adopt a very different approach from the exclusive, highly-tailored world of his Stephen Marks label. Clothes had to be faster-moving, more simply made, in more up-to-the-minute styles. But the reward would be much higher profits than he could get from classically designed coats and suits.

That first contact with Hong Kong paid off, too, for Marks began to order knitwear from there, and a few years later added menswear under the name French Connection No. 2. This side of the business mushroomed. Within two years of Marks first stepping off the plane at Bombay, imports outstripped the group's London output, and now dwarfs the Stephen Marks range.

But in the early days importing was tough, Marks admits. 'The big problem about dealing with India was timing,' he said. 'They did not understand that when we said delivery by Monday the 25th, we meant Monday the 25th and not a week later. In the beginning I was very soft. It's best not to understand too much about how things are made if you are buying, because then you have sympathy; you know how much work and effort has gone into the goods. If you can be cold-blooded about it, you can get a much better price. But I find it hard to be cold-blooded. I do not ever buy at the cheapest. But I want help from the supplier when we want to turn on the taps. If you have screwed down his price, then he is not exactly going to put himself out when you really need him.'

Marks added: 'I have still got five guys in India whom I found on my first trip. From little more than shacks they have built themselves up to have good businesses in their own right through supplying us. One makes 300,000 garments a month for us, and they have done it the way we want it. We have laid down standards which, after a bit of persuasion, they have followed. Just as the retailers have got to be able to rely on us, so we must be able to rely on our suppliers.'

However, Marks gradually realised that he could not entirely rely on the retailers who bought from him. He explained: 'We found it was all very well having a collection, but John Lewis or Debenhams would just buy the bits they wanted and display them in their shops alongside everything else in whatever way suited them. But if you have your own product, you have got to present it the way you want it.'

In 1973 the company had been asked to take space in the Oxford Street branch of Top Shop, and that gave Marks the idea that he might as well go the whole way and open his own outlets. 'Retail was the first conscious move I made, as opposed to something that just happened,' he said. 'We decided to buy a shop called Cane and put our own product in it. It was in Walton Street, near Sloane Square, and was just right for the Sloane Rangers. French Connection was quite trendy then, not as mass market as it is today. Now we have twenty shops in Britain. There are more than half-a-dozen in America, and a small one in Paris, converted from part of our showroom at Les Halles.'

French Connection's American connection was another of Marks' unplanned moves. Just as D'Alby persuaded him to go East, he had to be talked into going West in 1976 by a persistent bundle of energy called Michael Axelrod. 'One of the most significant developments was my meeting Michael Axelrod,' Marks declared. 'We were both showing in Paris. He phoned me to say that he had seen our collection in Paris and asked if we would be interested in doing a franchise in the US. I said I couldn't handle that. But he kept on at me. Eventually I suggested that he pop into my showroom next time he was in London. He was in my office at 11 o'clock the next morning, from New York. He didn't promise anything. But he impressed me because he was willing to get off his backside and come and see me. We never had anything in writing for God knows how long. It just started to grow more and more.'

Such was the size of the US market and the determination of Axelrod that by 1984 sales of French Connection clothes in America were greater than for the rest of the group. So they simply had to put something in writing. French Connection took a half share in Axelrod's business for $5,000,000; Axelrod went on the board of the British company and signed a five-year contract at $500,000 a year. No wonder Marks felt impelled to tell his shareholders: 'I have the greatest respect for Michael Axelrod's integrity and business skills, and I have no doubt that he will remain the driving force behind the company's continuing expansion in the United States.'

The dramatic impact that the US has had on French Connection's sales has been matched by the way it has opened Marks' eyes to the gap between the European and American approaches to business – a gap which is nearly as wide as the one Marks discovered between Britain and India.

Marks explained: 'The American way is so different from the English. To be successful in England is comparatively easy. To be successful in America is much more difficult. It's not just that the competition is tougher; they have much stronger ethical standards. If the delivery date is the 21st and you are only an hour late the order is cancelled. Then they come back and offer you half price. At first I couldn't handle this, but I soon learned that if the delivery date is the 31st I'd better make sure the goods are there by the 28th. And the seasons are so far ahead of anyone else's. The summer clothes are in the shops in December. The winter ranges are in the shops in May. I used to tell Michael not to be so silly, but finally I realised that we had to go along with it. They are heartless in business, which is a good thing, because it has made us more efficient. Nobody minds getting goods too early, but everybody minds getting goods late. They are much better at getting things done in America. Time is much more important.'

What the Americans have learned from Marks is that design sells. But design is the most elusive and intangible aspect of any fashion business, and one of the secrets of French Connection's success has been the way in which it has stayed in the forefront of fashion without coming a cropper at the hands of a fickle switch in taste.

Marks admitted: 'Fashion is changing more and more quickly. The world seems to be shrinking, and I see the same people in the business wherever I go: Paris, New York, Los Angeles, Tokyo. Everyone wants to go faster than the next person, and get in on the next fashion. And the retail stores in Britain have improved out of all recognition, with places like Next and the new Richard Shops. The choice is enormous. Our product has always sold. That has been our strength. We have always been in demand. Today we don't take so many chances. We have the experience to avoid many of the problems.'

Marks has always led the design team from the front. He likes to compare himself with the editor of a newspaper, hiring and firing designers, accepting or rejecting their work in the constant search for the next new look.

'I was in design from day one,' he said. 'There are two sorts of design. The first is totally creative, getting an idea from nowhere. The second, which is mine, gets inspiration from the things around you, from the streets, newspapers, a tablecloth. I was sitting in a toilet in Delhi, where I had been looking around for a particular type of brushed cotton. There in front of me, hanging on the door, was this glove for you to clean your shoes with. It was made of exactly the type of brushed cotton I wanted. I went out into the local market, found out where it came from and placed the order. Or I might see a sari on a lady and that will give me an idea for a line or a type of material.'

If that sounds delightfully hit or miss, do not be misled. Marks has almost from the start made a point of gathering talent around him. The chief designer is Nicole Farhi, who has worked for French Connection since 1978. She trained in Paris and worked as a freelance there, designing clothes and illustrating for the French fashion magazines *Elle* and *Marie Claire*. She lives in London with Marks and they have a daughter. In 1985 the group opened the first shops under the Nicole Farhi name, selling clothes designed and chosen exclusively for her. That has given the group a more upmarket label in the dress trade, and another fashion theme to sell through.

Further down the scale, however, the design team is constantly supplemented by freelances who might come in for only one season. Marks regularly trawls the best of the crop from the Royal College of Art for fresh recruits, who can only gain from a spell at a leading house like French Connection. Marks' job is to make the connection between what comes off the drawing board and what will sell.

He said: 'The designers travel a great amount and we are very aware of what is going on around us. But beyond that, it is no more possible to explain our consistency than you can explain the consistency of a successful newspaper. I'm conscious that as I grow older I am moving further away from our target audience, but we try to counter that by bringing in younger people and listening to them.' So far, he has not put a foot wrong on that side of the business.

Marks admits to having had something of a happy-go-lucky approach to the business in the early days. Designing, making and selling were all that mattered. 'We unconsciously became successful,' he said. 'It never occurred to me where I wanted to go; I just wanted to keep it moving, keep going.'

This inevitably left some loose ends trailing along until there was time to deal with them. Together, three of these loose ends dragged the group down from a £544,000 profit to a £68,000 loss in the three years to the end of January, 1982.

The company had chronic problems making a profit in France, where over 700 different retailers had to be served alongside the big chains like Galeries Lafayette and Au Printemps. As this was coming to a head, Marks bought a chain of shops which took two years to pull out of the red. In 1981, Marks achieved his ambition of emulating his old employer, Sheraton, by installing a computer to control stocks and feed back management information, but this too went sour until Marks recruited an accountant, Michael Shen from the firm of Ernst and Whinney, to scrap everything and start from scratch.

The costs of scrapping the original computer system and buying an IBM System 34 added to the short-term problems. But by the time the company went public in October 1983, Marks was able to convince the City that these difficulties were in the past. Going public added to French Connection's credibility, not least with shop landlords, as well as putting a value on Marks' personal fortune.

Marks said of the losses recorded in 1981: 'My biggest mistake was letting somebody else tell me who I should employ. In France we employed somebody who had nothing to do with the aspirations of this business. I should have had nothing to do with him. But we brought in Stuart Selwyn from Marks and Spencer, and he reorganised the whole French operation. We employ people on the basis that they have to perform and in return we have to perform. If someone is genuinely trying and we have put him in a job he cannot do, we take the most sympathetic line we can and try to find him something else to do. But if he is not trying, he gets out of the door immediately.' Happily, that has happened only rarely at French Connection, and they still have some of the staff Marks started with as a 23-year-old.

The company employs about 600 people, and is still small enough for Marks to exert a strong personal influence. 'I believe in dictatorship,' he said. 'If it's a day-to-day question, then the person running the French operation will make the decisions in France, whoever is running the retail side will make the decisions about retail, and so on. If it is something more long-term, then I deal with it. I think that too many cooks spoil the broth. You have got to move very quickly.'

Marks has been shrewd enough to move slowly into his big opportunities, in the Far East and the United States, whilst moving quickly enough not to let his mistakes get out of hand. It will be fascinating to see how the business develops. Although there are one or two obvious gaps in the company, such as mail order and possibly some attack on the teenage market, the big strategic question must still concern the US.

French Connection's success across the Atlantic has already led Marks to bring his US distributor under the parent company's umbrella. The American accent could become considerably stronger yet within the next few years, as the French Connection chain of ships expands over there, spanning the east and west coasts. By doing so, it at least partly insulates Marks from the frenetic business of selling to the big US stores, and gives him greater control over the way the French Connection image is handled. That distinctive but elusive feel is the group's most precious asset.

Robert Maxwell

It is all too easy to lapse into caricature in any attempt to convey the flavour of Robert Maxwell's career: Czech peasant turned war hero; socialist millionaire; briefly a Labour member of parliament; then the man the City of London loved to hate, who in the last reel achieved his ambition to run a national newspaper. All those statements are facts, as far as they go. But they go next to nowhere in terms of explaining what makes Robert Maxwell tick – and it is highly unlikely that we have seen anything like the last reel in the metaphorical film of his extraordinary life, barring some unforeseen stroke of fate.

To the public at large, he is best known as the man who runs the *Daily Mirror* and its sister papers, the *Daily Record*, *Sunday Mirror*, *Sunday People*, *Sunday Mail* and *The Sporting Life*. After his family's master company in Britain, Pergamon, bought Mirror Group Newspapers from Reed International in July 1984, he made sure there was no mistake about who was in charge. Within weeks he had started intervening in the coal dispute; a few months later he was flying to Ethiopia and Sudan with his readers' famine relief fund; and, amidst all this, his name and face were fronting the Mirror's millionaire bingo competition.

Not even his best friends would call Maxwell a shy man, and he has clearly enjoyed the recognition which has gone with the job of being a Fleet Street press baron. But away from the hype it has to be remembered that the Mirror is only one piece in the business mosaic which Maxwell has been assembling for more than thirty years. That business is all about communications and information technology in every conceivable form, linked so that each can feed off the others.

Pergamon is one of the western world's most important scientific and technical publishers. It has a controlling interest in British Printing and Communication Corporation, the biggest printer in Europe. Maxwell has a stake in independent television, and has been putting himself in a powerful position in the embryonic British cable television business through the takeover of Rediffusion Cable.

Maxwell explained: 'I expect the combination of Pergamon, BPCC, Mirror Group and Rediffusion Cable to be one of ten surviving global publishing companies. Once you understand that, you understand what I have been driving at all these years. We are where the oil industry was at the beginning of this century, when there were thousands of companies going round with cans of kerosene and filling them at the wellhead. Immediately after the Second World War, all these oil companies were rationalised, and came down to seven or ten giants. It will be the same in publishing.'

Despite his confidence, Maxwell has a long way to go before he can claim to have fulfilled his grand ambition. But there is little doubt that he saw the shape of things to come well in advance of most of his present-day rivals. The date can be fixed more or less exactly at August 6, 1945 – the day the atomic bomb fell on Hiroshima. He recalled: 'Whilst thinking about what I was going to be doing, I remember being very impressed by the way the Americans got the Japanese to surrender through the use of the nuclear weapon. I was very impressed that scientists, by their knowledge, could bring Japan to its knees when we had all assumed that the war would go on for years, and that it would be an almighty struggle to win in the Far East. I decided I wanted to be of service to science. I did not have the training or education to do so directly, but scientists are not like any other breed. They are not tied to any one nation because they must build on one another's knowledge. They must be open, unless they are working on classified projects, so that they can test their ideas on one another. There are not just British nuclear physicists or Russian nuclear physicists, they are all part of the same community and the best of them want to communicate with one another. When I started Pergamon I introduced the international dimension into scientific publishing.'

Possibly Maxwell also saw a lesson for his future business tactics in the dropping of the atomic bomb on an unsuspecting opponent, but his immediate thought was of getting out of the army. He had had a distinguished war, starting in the Czech underground at the age of fifteen and finishing with the rank of Captain in the British Army after being awarded the Military Cross for bravery in the field in Holland.

'I learned a lot in the army,' he said. 'After the war they offered me a regular commission, but the peacetime army was not my scene. I was about to take up a job as export manager, when I was asked to go to the press department of the Foreign Office in Berlin. I went, but left after a disagreement. The Russians were kidnapping people off the streets if they knew anything about rockets. I attacked the Russians in the newspapers I controlled through my position in the press office, because I was disgusted at this illegal and barbarous activity. The Foreign Office were highly embarrassed at this – it came at a time when Britain and Russia were trying to be friends – and I found myself being offered a promotion to Schleswig-Holstein, to get me out of the way. I said no, and left.'

That was in 1947. In the two years after Hiroshima, Maxwell had begun cultivating contacts who might prove useful to him in a civilian career. Being in the press office of an occupying power opened doors for him in the German publishing world. Among the contacts he made was Julius Springer of Springer Verlag, the top German scientific publisher. He offered Maxwell a job as an agent for his export business.

Maxwell recalled: 'I had always decided that I would run my own business when I left the army. It was a natural decision for me because I think by looking for concepts. I always ask myself, how does the ring close? What's around the corner? In London, other people look at the map if they want to get around. I say, where do I want to get to and what is the quickest way of getting there. Street maps are not for me. I see the topography of a situation very quickly. I do not know where I picked it up, but it was of tremendous use in the fighting in the war.'

Springer must have been impressed by his new young recruit, for Maxwell soon brought him an important deal involving the British government. One of the spoils of the Second World War for the victors in Europe was the huge cache of German classified material, much of it relating to such dramatic but until then secret technical developments as rocketry. While the Russians and the Americans were, in their different ways, trying to lure German scientists to their respective countries, Britain found itself in possession of an unimaginable store of research documents.

Churchill, realising the potential gains to be had from this windfall, set up an Enemy Publications Committee, known as EPCOM, to organise it and bring it back to Britain to see what benefits could be culled for military, commercial or industrial purposes. The designated agent was His Majesty's Stationery Office. They collected huge warehouses of the research in Hamburg. But they were too slow about shipping it.

In 1947, Ernest Bevin, Britain's Foreign Secretary, and Secretary of State James F. Byrnes of the United States concluded an agreement to create a joint Anglo-American Zone in Germany. After that, it was forbidden to export anything from there without paying for it and obtaining a licence which had to be agreed by the two nations. This put HMSO, as a government body, in a difficult position.

Maxwell, fresh from his press office job, was asked to import these documents for the Government in his private capacity, and got the licence to do so. He did not have enough experience to carry out such a major undertaking on his own. But new though he was to the commercial world, he made sure that he got his share of the proceeds by putting the deal through a company called Lange Maxwell and Springer.

At this stage Maxwell was forming a business base in Britain. He was engaged in a variety of import-export deals, of which importing German periodicals for prisoners of war was only a part. Gradually he shifted the emphasis wholly over to publishing.

Julius Springer had a 49 per cent stake in Butterworth Springer, jointly with the British Butterworth publishing company. Maxwell bought Butterworth Springer with help from Hambros Bank, the City merchant bank which acted for Springer, and through what Maxwell describes as 'a small loan from my family in America'. Mrs Maxwell has said that the couple also received financial assistance from her father, who had been a wealthy Lyons silk merchant. In 1951 Butterworth Springer changed its name to Pergamon Press, as that was where Julius Springer had found the colophon of the goddess Athena which the firm had been using, and still uses, as its logo. In a low-key but literal sense, Maxwell had arrived on the British business scene.

He began the process of making and consolidating his contacts with the scientific community, using his undoubted charm and his facility with languages. He quickly realised that he had stumbled on a commercial situation which had several unusual features.

In the first place, in scientific publishing his customers and the suppliers of his raw material were one and the same. Secondly, this audience was not itself commercial. The scientists were not looking to make a financial profit. This had a considerable bearing on any agreements between them or their librarians and Maxwell, as did the third factor: these people were not in the main spending their own money, and indeed their organisations typically obtained their revenue from governments or educational foundations.

Fourthly, Maxwell discovered that he could in effect create very narrow but very powerful monopolies through starting scientific journals which became the accepted forum for exchange of information in a given discipline. As Maxwell established confidence in the Pergamon imprint, it in turn became accepted as a serious scientific publisher, and more importantly one which was sympathetic to the interests and concerns of the academics themselves.

Academics began coming to Maxwell to persuade him to launch a new title in their particular field. It was never difficult to find out if there was enough demand for a new title: a few phone calls to the right universities round the world would decide the question, assuming that Maxwell's gut reaction did not give him the answer instantly.

He explained with some glee: 'At Pergamon I set up a perpetual financing machine through advance subscriptions as well as the profits on the sales themselves. It is a cash generator twice over. It's no use trying to compete with me, because I publish the authoritative journal in each field. I charge far more than anyone else for the subscriptions, and I not only pay nothing for the material – Nobel Laureates queue up to pay me handsomely for the privilege of having their work published. I can charge high prices, £1,000 a year or more in some cases, because I am dealing in high-penalty information. People must have it. If you are building a chemical plant and you do not happen to know about the latest development in that area, the mistake could cost you £10 million. So people will pay £1,000. It's worth it to them.'

It would be wrong to give the impression that this happened overnight. But during the 1950s Maxwell put the pieces in place, building his catalogue of journals and books, and acquiring printing capacity. In parallel with the development of his business career, he was also nurturing his political career.

Whilst his belief in a form of socialism is undoubtedly sincere, his growing relationship with the opposition Labour Party at that time was helpful in two ways. It added to his credibility among the academics as someone who had wider horizons than the normal run of businesssmen. And the Labour connection would be a valuable commercial asset when the party was returned to power. Indeed, he was himself elected to parliament in the general election of October 1964, when Harold Wilson became prime minister for the first time.

That crowned an important year for Maxwell. Only a few months earlier, Pergamon had gone public on the London stock market and Maxwell could plausibly claim to be one of the few bridges between the new Labour government and the business lobby, presenting the arguments of one side to the other by turns. And Pergamon's scientific bias chimed in perfectly with Wilson's call for a 'white-hot technological revolution' in Britain, to be exemplified by greater emphasis on the teaching of science subjects in schools. Wilson, who had gained a brilliant first at Oxford, was also committed to spending more on higher education. All this helped to feed Maxwell's business ambitions.

It is worth bearing in mind, in view of later events, that the prospectus for Pergamon's stock market flotation spelled out how Maxwell saw the company in terms of information retrieval in the broadest sense. This would inevitably involve computerised databanks, and equally inescapable would be the need for Pergamon to have control of a wide range of media.

Maxwell has had several setbacks along the route to the degree of control he seeks. Between 1968 and 1984 he tried and failed to take over *The Sun,* the *News of the World,* Express Newspapers, Times Newspapers, the *Observer* and John Waddington, the printing and packaging company which produces playing cards, Monopoly, Cluedo and other games. In 1975 he tried to launch the *Scottish Daily News* as a workers' co-operative, but it had to be closed within a few months.

This catalogue should be seen as a testimony to Maxwell's stamina in refusing to be beaten. It is also a barometer of his standing with the business community, Whitehall and the closed world of the City establishment, along with the Leasco affair between 1969 and 1974, the rescue of British Printing Corporation in 1981 and the coup three years later to buy Mirror Group Newspapers.

Maxwell admits that the Leasco affair was one of his two biggest mistakes. The other was the 1955 collapse of Simpkin Marshall, the book wholesaler.

Maxwell explained: 'Simpkin Marshall was a book wholesaling firm. At that time, Pitmans did a lot of the wholesaling for the book trade, but I tried to get the publishers together and do it cheaper. But they did not want to know, and it cost me £250,000 to close it down. It taught me never to go into any business where the margins are controlled for you.'

That is a drastic simplification of what was a complex business collapse. Pitman, the company which is world-famous for its shorthand system, owned Simpkin Marshall but was losing money on it. Maxwell took control of Simpkin mainly by agreeing to repay Pitman the money Simpkin owed it. Soon afterwards he tried to give Simpkin another outlet by buying the British Book Center in New York, which was in the end unable to pay the trade debts it ran up on Simpkins' account.

Back in Britain, the new proprietor set Simpkin up in its own London headquarters in Marylebone, called Maxwell House. But he was unable to break the publishers' stranglehold on him: the shop price of books was and is fixed by the publishers, and in the end neither they nor the booksellers were willing to yield enough of their profit margin to give Simpkin a living.

Simpkin failed owing £556,000. The Official Receiver was

critical of the way it had been run. He said: 'It appears doubtful whether the company was at any time solvent. The directors concerned were at fault in acquiring the Marylebone premises and financing the British Book Center at a time when the company was insolvent, without making satisfactory arrangements for the introduction of sufficient further capital. Moreover, as the company was unable to obtain a larger margin between publishers' prices and the company's selling prices and as its overhead expenses continued to increase, it would seem that the directors concerned should have considered and decided upon liquidation at a much earlier date.'

It was not the last time that Maxwell would be taken to task in an official report. It also focused his way of doing business in the eyes of the publishing community of which he was part. Some of the top names in the business were creditors of Simpkin, and they were repaid less than 20p in the pound. But, as Maxwell wryly pointed out, that also reflected the high prices they insisted on charging him.

The memories lingered. Maxwell admitted to the *Sunday Express* in 1968: 'I am probably the most unpopular publisher among publishers. But I pay no attention to these matters. I don't care whether I'm popular or unpopular. Naturally I don't relish it, I don't seek it. But I've no time to bother about it. It's largely sour grapes.' An unnamed rival added: 'Maxwell tends to think everyone else a fool. He's disliked by publishers because he keeps trying to take over the lot of us. He has no modesty and eventually I think he'll overreach himself.'

In the next year that final remark was to seem ominously prophetic. Maxwell was up to his neck in an epic battle which it is agreed by all concerned would have finished the career of any other businessman, and would have killed some: the Leasco affair. However much blame is attached to him, it is impossible not to acknowledge his determination, his persistence and and above all his resilience in the face of what at times appeared to be overwhelming odds. He entered the affair as a Member of Parliament and chairman of a successful public company. Before it was over, control of Pergamon had been wrested from him for more than four years, and it was another six years before he re-entered the public arena in business. He lost his Parliamentary seat in the Labour election defeat of 1970.

Nowadays, Maxwell is terse about the US-based Leasco Data Processing and its bouncy chairman, Saul Steinberg. He said: 'Steinberg came to me. He had thousands of computers lying idle, and I had thousands of items which needed to be computerised. It looked an utterly logical and natural fit. But he didn't have the resources.' Steinberg would, of course, strongly refute any such suggestion. He made an agreed £25 million takeover bid for Pergamon in June 1969 but withdrew after two months, citing doubts over Pergamon's profit forecast, the trading links between Pergamon and private companies owned by Maxwell and his family, and the performance of International Learning Systems Corporation, an encyclopaedia business then owned jointly by Pergamon and British Printing Corporation. Maxwell was voted off the board and into the wilderness.

The withdrawal of a public takeover bid does not happen often, but it is rarely more than a matter of some embarrassment for those involved. What made this one different was that in the meantime Leasco had bought a considerable number of Pergamon shares on the stock market. By the time Steinberg decided to pull out, Leasco was Pergamon's biggest shareholder. The American company had a 38 per cent stake, compared with Maxwell's 28 per cent. And Leasco could not sell without incurring a huge loss. It had paid up to nearly 185p a share, the value of the original bid, but after the deal was called off the price naturally collapsed. It was not just that the deal was aborted; it was the reasons which frightened the stock market, and were to be the cause of Maxwell's crucifixion over the years that followed.

Innocuous-sounding in themselves, Leasco's reasons for withdrawing, cited with the advice of N. M. Rothschild, possibly the City's most respected merchant bank, implied the most serious criticism of Maxwell and the auditors of Pergamon's accounts. The ensuing row brought home to the investing public the fact that the reckoning of a company's profit is very much a matter of opinion and estimation, and the result is worthless unless outsiders are told what assumptions the exercise is based on.

Most laymen automatically assume that a business can make a

profit only when it sells something. But accountants, with the support of the Inland Revenue, accept that if the value of unsold stock has risen, then that should be included in the profit. Maxwell argued that the back numbers of Pergamon's scientific journals were rising all the time, because of their scarcity value. If a university decided to take an interest in a field covered by a Pergamon journal, then it virtually had to buy the back numbers to know what had been discovered in that activity.

What gave rise to unease at the time was that the value Maxwell put on these stocks was in some cases verified only by sales to the private companies owned by him or his family. Nearly a third of Pergamon's 1968 profit came from one such transaction. Maxwell claimed that all these deals were at arm's length on a commercial basis. But trading between a public company and its directors' private interests is fraught with difficulty, and it was a mistake to let them become so significant to Pergamon's fortunes. Ironically, the explosion in technical publishing in the past fifteen years has been so great that even Maxwell's valuations turned out to be far too conservative.

But for several years the mud stuck. It stuck because in those days his statements were frequently open to more than one interpretation, and it was the unexpected version which often turned out to be the one that mattered. There were too many surprises, not all of them pleasant, for the people on the other side of the negotiating table. 'I have never gone back on my word, or broken it,' Maxwell says today. But he did not consider himself bound by the City's unwritten rules, and that was regarded in some quarters as a deep affront.

Instead, Maxwell took it all as part of the cut and thrust of doing business, and was surprised when others did not do likewise. To some extent he has shared this misjudgment with Sir James Goldsmith and Roland 'Tiny' Rowland, two other foreign-born entrepreneurs who have had great success in Britain only in the midst of deep controversy.

Arguably, in the past decade Maxwell has done more to adapt to the British business environment than the other two. But as the storm broke in the late summer of 1969 he lashed out, accusing certain people in the City of 'sharpening their knives against me'.

The dispute very quickly escalated. Leasco complained to the City Takeover Panel. The Panel decided to make an example of Maxwell by passing the case to the Department of Trade and Industry, which ordered an inquiry by a Queen's Counsel and a leading accountant. An interim report of that inquiry dismissed Maxwell as unfit to run a public company, but he angrily claimed that he had not been given a fair hearing and set a precedent by taking the official investigators to court. The judge found substantially in Maxwell's favour, but the damage had been done.

While the inquiry dragged on, Pergamon was sinking rapidly. It was being run by neutral figures acceptable to the City, but who understandably could not match Maxwell's feel for the delicate business of handling prickly academic egos. Leasco could not stomach the idea of Maxwell returning to the board. Everyone was locked into this impossible situation because the Stock Exchange had suspended dealings in the shares. Eventually, City investment fund managers insisted that Maxwell release them from their predicament by making a bid for Pergamon, which he did at 12½p a share. If they were requoted in 1985, the price would be in the region of £20 or £30.

After he had regained control of Pergamon, most people in the City thought that that was the end of Robert Maxwell as a public figure. But they were wrong. He ploughed back Pergamon's rapidly reviving profits into the computerisation scheme that would have been provided by Leasco, and sunk much of the rest into buying Government stock. Apart from underlining his financial probity, this was also an excellent way to find new friends in the City; there were once again large fees and commissions to be made out of acting for Pergamon. Grieveson Grant, one of the biggest stockbroking firms, and the leading merchant bank Hill Samuel were among those taking instructions from Maxwell. He retained the services of Cooper Bros., the top accountancy firm which had been called in to audit Pergamon's books during the crisis. They continued to put their name to the company's annual accounts, which did Maxwell's image no harm.

The turning point in his public rehabilitation came in 1980, when he went into the stock market and bought 29 per cent of British Printing Corporation, the largest printer in the country and

Maxwell's former partner in the encyclopaedia business. The board of BPC asked the Office of Fair Trading to stand by the Department of Trade inspectors' verdict that Maxwell was 'not in our opinion a person who can be relied on to exercise proper stewardship of a publicly quoted company', but the silence was stony.

BPC continued to lose money heavily and in the following year its own bank, National Westminster, called on Maxwell to take control. The stock market listing was retained, so with the approval of the Stock Exchange and one of the major high-street banks Maxwell was indeed exercising stewardship of a public company again.

Under the new name of British Printing and Communication Corporation, the operation has since gone from strength to strength. Yet Maxwell's relations with the City remain ambivalent. In 1984 some of the institutional shareholders in Reed International put pressure on the board to sell Mirror Group Newspapers to Maxwell rather than float it on the stock market. But within a few months other City investors snubbed Maxwell's attempt to take over Waddington, his second seige of that company in just over a year.

In some quarters of the Establishment, Maxwell never will be fully accepted. Doubts will persist as long as there are potential conflicts of interests among his businesses: in BPCC there are public shareholders, Pergamon is owned by a Liechtenstein trust and he has a personal stake in other activities. While the law now provides for closer scrutiny of dealings between businesses run by the same person, the very complexity of the Maxwell empire is a source of unease. He has made enemies too easily, and sometimes underestimates the extent to which he can wound. Possibly he expects everyone else to be as resilient as he is. The tragedy is that his style has been in danger of obscuring his achievements.

Pergamon was a brilliant creation, which he has exploited to a degree that no other publisher in Britain could have contemplated. In BPCC and the Mirror Group he has acquired control of two businesses where costs had been allowed to billow unchecked. He said: 'At BPCC the unions had insisted on vast over-manning and the management was incompetent. I reduced expenses by

£600,000 a week. After that, it was not difficult to make money out of that business!' His methods are simple: the spending process is slowed dramatically by the rule that a whole range of decisions must be approved by his signature. This can include every employee hired, every executive trip abroad, every piece of overtime worked and every sum spent over as little as £1,000.

The Mirror Group has been subjected to similar rigours. But both companies are in highly competitive industries, and the long-term question is whether Maxwell can convert them to electronic publishing and knit them successfully into the Pergamon pattern.

Maxwell explained: 'Increasingly, people cannot afford to wait for the slow process of producing printed material. The cost of computing has come down so immensely that Pergamon can store a massive amount of information and have it instantly available. We want to get involved with anything to do with information. My aim has been that all problems in life, except those at the very forefront of knowledge, can be solved, but only if they are in a form for decision makers to make use of. The difficulty lies in finding that information, and how to package it in a form that the individual can use to increase earnings, or pleasure, or education. It's the educating of people and putting it to them in a form they can use that's important. Most people are put off by huge books. They don't know where to start looking for something, and they find it hard work. We can enrich them, simply by making it easier for them to get hold of the information, whether on computer, or cable or wherever.'

He envisages people being able to respond to an advertisement in the *Daily Mirror* though cable television, and buying goods on mail order in the same way instead of leafing through a bulky catalogue. Just as Pergamon's academic subscribers can have instant access to a databank, why shouldn't the man in the street be able to dial up a Mirror information service?

Now in his early sixties, Maxwell is in a race against time if he is to put together the ambitious information-handling giant he has in mind. There is no time to develop it by organic growth. He must grow by takeovers, and on an international scale they must be paid for in cash. At the level he wishes to operate, the stakes come very high indeed. But the moral of Maxwell's success throughout his career is that single-mindedness and persistence win in the end.

Gerald Ronson

Gerald Ronson makes few compromises in life. Born in Paddington, west London, he speaks his mind and expects others to do likewise. It is, however, a fact of life that not everyone does likewise, so Ronson has trudged a long, hard road to persuade the world that he is here to stay. The message has got through; the world, or at least that part of it with money to lend, has been beating a path to his door.

Heron International, Ronson's master company, ranks as the second biggest private company in Britain, where it owns petrol stations, property and housebuilding under the Heron name, the H. R. Owen Rolls-Royce concession, and National Insurance and Guarantee Corporation. Overseas, the group has extensive property interests in France, Belgium, Switzerland and North America, as well as a US bank and one of America's most successful savings and loan associations, roughly the equivalent of a British building society. With all this activity, Heron is fast catching Britain's biggest private company, Littlewoods of stores and football pools fame. 'If only I'd had the good years they've had in the past to build my business on – the mind boggles,' Ronson said. 'Remember, I've had to do it through a recession.'

It is a feature of the Ronson conversational style that he feels compelled to remind his audience of how much he has done and how much he has had to struggle. The years of having to prove himself, to everyone from his father downwards, have left their mark and still keep him striving despite the fact that Heron's assets are worth well over half a billion pounds.

But, given his upbringing, that defensiveness is hardly surprising. His grandparents were Russian immigrants who fled the pogroms in the early years of this century. The family skill was cabinet-making, but Ronson inherited the family physique: his father, Henry, was an amateur light-heavyweight champion in the 1930s and Ronson's burly frame could easily be taken for a boxer's today.

Ronson was born in 1939. His father was clearly a vital influence on his life, and has been an important driving force behind his business success. 'For the first 24 years of my life, until I began to understand what he was doing, there was no one in the world who could wind me up like my father,' Ronson admitted. 'I worked as hard as I could, and still he wanted more. I was a millionaire by the age of 23, and that was when it was a lot harder to make a million than it is today, and still he would have a go at me. I would say, "What do you want, do I have to move a mountain with my bare hands? What am I supposed to prove?" '

But that only served to emphasise how close they were. When Ronson was older, and could sit down and talk things over with his father, Henry would tell Gerald, 'I knew you had it in you, and I had to bring it out.' Gerald left school at fourteen and a half 'although the story books say fifteen'. He said: 'I hated school. I couldn't wait to get out. I loathed every day I had to take the bus to school. I can remember saying to myself at the age of nine, "This is a waste of time. What do I want with all this?" I hated the way we were treated like sheep, and the teachers' attitude to us. I admit I was a bit of a rascal. I was good at sport, and arithmetic – it wasn't called maths in those days. I had a sharp mind. But I remember one of the teachers, who I really hated, saying to me "You'll never be anything, Ronson, because you're good for nothing", and that made me determined to prove him wrong.'

As soon as he got out he went to work in his father's furniture business, working long hours, 7 a.m. to 8.30 p.m. Mondays to Fridays, 7 a.m. to 1 p.m. on Saturdays, and then often going in on Sundays and sitting in on meetings. 'You had to get in early if you didn't want my father on your back, so it paid to get in at five to seven,' said Ronson. 'And if you enjoyed it, as I did, you willingly stayed until half past eight at night.' The habit has never left him. He still works twelve hours a day, six days a week.

At those Sunday morning meetings, which still take place at Heron, the young Gerald sat and watched and listened, absorbing what was going on. He recalled: 'When I was young I was a very good listener. That's how I learnt about the business. I'm still a good listener when I want to be, which isn't so often nowadays. But if someone's got something intelligent to say, or I want to get some information from them, then I listen.' Before long, he and his father were running the family business in tandem.

In 1956 they decided to get out of the furniture business. Ronson explained: 'We felt it was a clapped-out business that had no prospects. We were making enough to give us a living and £25,000 a year profit on top. It wasn't bad for those days, the equivalent of about £150,000 today. But it was never going to go very far. And then we built a new factory for £100,000 which we sold for £198,500. My father said, "That's as much as we make in four years, working thirteen hours a day and employing 350 people." So we closed down the furniture business and went into property. We found jobs for all the furniture workers. I still bump into some of them today: one of them manages the Crush Bar at the Royal Opera House, Covent Garden.'

As many property tycoons will testify, the early years in that business tend to be slow, gathering pace only on the back of past increases in values. So it was with the Ronsons. They started with £1,000,000 and nine years later the property portfolio had grown to £4,500,000, mainly through developing shops, blocks of flats and industrial estates round the country. Then they formed Heron – an abbreviation of Henry Ronson's name – and Gerald made a move which proved every bit as important as his father's decision to get out of furniture. He got into petrol stations.

It was a natural extension of the property business, taking advantage of the rapid growth in mass motoring in the early 1960s. In fact, so popular had it become that at busy times they found they could not take the money quickly enough. Drivers would turn up, see the queues and go on to the next filling station. Through-put is vitally important to any retail operation, but the big oil companies hardly noticed the problem because they saw their petrol stations as merely an extension of their mainstream business, oil refining and distribution. Ronson had no such luxury, so he had every incentive to develop a radical new way of selling petrol which he had spotted in the US: self-service.

Ronson was the first in the UK to introduce the self-service concept in petrol stations. 'The layout you see all over the world today, the four pumps with a shop at the side, seems so simple you'd say that it's obvious, anyone could do that – and you may be right,' Ronson admitted. 'But the fact is that we were the first in this country, and the major oil companies would acknowledge that.'

It turned out to be Heron's engine of growth. He would buy the site, get a business going, and sell it on for a capital profit. It was a vital source of cash flow during the difficult days of the property market in the mid-1970s. 'That business provided us with the fuel to go out and buy other businesses at a time when it was almost impossible to sell properties,' said Ronson. Over the years, Heron has owned about 500 forecourts, but is now down to about sixty. 'There isn't the money in petrol retailing these days,' he added. But the trading in the stations themselves has brought the group substantial profits. They also brought Ronson an early reputation for toughness. He started a system of charging the filling station attendants for any petrol shortages which showed up. 'I'm not MI5,' he explained. 'I can't go snooping on them. But if someone is taking £50 out of the till, he's taking £50 out of my pocket, and I'm not having that. So if there's anything missing, I knock it off the wages of the people who were on that shift. Then they can sort it out amongst themselves if they want to. I tell you one thing: there are plenty of crooks in the petrol business, but they don't tend to come and work for us.' The crooks must be having a hard time, for Heron is by no means alone in adopting this policy.

Those years dealing in shops, offices, houses and petrol stations gave Ronson the key to his business: property and cash flow. Property gave him something tangible, something real to hold on to. It had value. Certainly, that value could rise and fall, but if you were conservative enough in your own mind about what it was worth, property would not let you down. But it was also important not to borrow too much to buy property, because that committed the investor to handing money to the banks before he could be sure he was going to collect enough in rent. In the late 1960s and early 1970s, many businesses borrowed heavily to get into property, on the assumption that values would keep on rising. But in 1974 they got their come-uppance: the market crashed. Ronson, though, sold some properties for at least what he had paid for them, kept his head down and survived. After that, he knew he could survive any financial hurricane, as long as he was cautious enough.

By now Heron had the muscle to expand. The petrol business reached comfortably out to the garage trade, where Ronson could combine business with his love of cars. Aside from H. R. Owen, the group today sells BL, Vauxhall, Fiat, Volvo, Subaru, Talbot-Peugeot, Massey-Ferguson, Suzuki and Lancia.

The other important activity Ronson has taken Heron into is financial services. The group has an insurance company in London and a fast-growing savings and loan association in Tucson, Arizona. In the UK, his National Insurance and Guarantee Corporation is one of the biggest privately-owned motor insurers.

He went into insurance because he then regarded it as a soft industry, poorly run in the main and badly sold. He cited Hambro Life and Legal and General as rare exceptions to this view. He wants five per cent of the UK motor insurance business. 'The cash flow from that would be just amazing,' he pointed out. 'Insurance is like sophisticated bookmaking: if you get the odds right, you can't lose. I say what I want the policies to do and the experts work it out.' However, Ronson has had to cope with the fact that, in common with some of the leaders in the field, National Insurance and Guarantee has been losing money on its motor business, thanks to the number of claims and the ever-increasing cost of repairs. Like the others, though, it makes up for this with income from investing the policyholders' premiums.

Ronson has not been slow to leap on the bandwagon carrying a long list of British businesses into the ever-tantalising US market. He spends several days a month over there, and shares the ambition of many of his compatriots to have half their profits stemming from America within a few years, mainly from property and financial services. He has lit on Tucson, Arizona, as the place to base his operations, because Arizona is apparently keen to attract foreign investment and Tucson is one of the fastest-growing cities in the US, even though a quarter of the households are occupied by what are known locally as 'retirees'.

Tucson is also the home of Pima Savings, a savings and loan

association which Ronson bought in 1980 and by 1984 claimed to be Arizona's fastest-growing major financial institution. Ronson keeps a very low profile in the annual report of Pima. He features modestly in one group photograph of the company's directors, and you have to comb the small print of the report carefully to discover that Pima is ultimately controlled by Heron, which is not itself identified any further. 'They don't like that kind of thing in Arizona, the Americans have got to be the top dogs. They don't want to believe that us poor Brits could run anything,' Ronson said with a smile.

That thought gave extra zest to one of his best coups in recent years, when through Pima he paid $76 million for 12,500 acres of land around Tucson from the estate of the late eccentric billionaire, Howard Hughes. Ronson had the land valued at over $200 million and within a few months had sold 2,000 acres for $55 million. 'And that wasn't just the best land,' Ronson added.

Heron also owns Western American Financial Corporation, a mortgage bank and insurance broking company based in nearby Phoenix. A US insurance arm would be another logical addition to Ronson's shopping list.

In both Britain and the US Ronson has been developing another trading activity, in the rapidly emerging business of distributing video cassette tapes. In 1983 Heron bought a north London company, Videoform, which sells and leases the tapes to retailers using an up-to-date computerised booking and logging system. Later that year Ronson acquired a parallel business operating out of Los Angeles in California, Media Home Entertainments, which has a massive duplicating facility and distributes video tapes internationally. Ronson has started his own film production unit to supply raw material for the video market and has an electronics offshoot marketing the hardware of TV, audio and video systems.

Yet until 1981 Heron was best known in the British business community for the fact that it was hardly known at all. 'At that stage it was just another of those very private businesses you see dotted around the place,' said one stockbroker ruefully, 'and about all we knew was that it owned petrol stations and was run by that big fellow with a chip on his shoulder.'

But by the end of that year Ronson had sprung into prominence with a much-publicised battle for Associated Communications Corporation, the entertainments group created by the rumbustious Lord Lew Grade, which owned ATV, formerly the Midlands television station. The bidding had been started at £35 million by Robert Holmes a' Court, an Australian who had been brought on to the ACC board by Lord Grade. After a couple of months and two intervening bids by Ronson, the Australian raised the stakes to £60 million. Ronson called it a day, saying 'We played poker and Mr Holmes a' Court won.' But the City had been given the clear message that Ronson was in the market as a potential take-over bidder. Before long, people were bringing ideas for deals to him.

In 1982 he brushed against Rank Organisation, then desperately searching for ways out of its financial difficulties. Ronson offered to buy Rank's franchise for Xerox copiers, but was turned down. He did not relish taking on the whole of the troubled Rank business, and backed away. Then, early the following year, he demonstrated his new-found clout by teaming up with some of the biggest investment groups in the country, including the Post Office and National Coal Board pension funds, to mount an ambitious £200 million bid for UDS Group, the clothing stores company which then owned Richard Shops and John Collier. Again he was outbid and again he took a handsome profit on his shareholding. The point was driven home that he was not going to be lured by the excitement of an auction into paying any more than he intended.

Ronson makes no secret of the fact that he is on the lookout for businesses which are asset-rich, straightforward and give a good cash flow. 'There is no limit to the number of badly-managed British companies, but we will not pay prices which reflect inflated Stock Exchange values. I'm not in the business of paying a lot for goodwill,' he has said.

In the meantime a long list of the City's bankers and brokers have been calling at Ronson's head office opposite Madame Tussaud's waxworks in London to pay their respects and try and tempt him into sampling some of their smart financial schemes. The most obvious would be for Heron to have its shares quoted on the London Stock Exchange as he could pay for takeover bids by issuing new shares instead of handing over hard cash. But Ronson has set his face against this. 'We don't want to hand out funny money to pay for companies. We prefer to use the real stuff,' he said.

As it is, sixty per cent of Heron's shares are committed to the Ronson Charitable Foundation and the rest are in trust. 'I've got no capital in the business,' he explained. 'I'm not going to leave any to my children. They won't be short of a bob, but they won't have a big stake in Heron. I don't believe in it. I started with nothing. I pay myself a good salary, enough to be comfortable, but then we don't pay dividends. We can plough all our earnings back into the company and worry about long-term capital appreciation and long-term planning. We consider it a great luxury to be private.' In 1983 Ronson received £446,000 from Heron, then one of the highest incomes in the land.

Despite his desire to stick to the simple life, Ronson has been persuaded into one or two stock market forays, and he has been toying with other plans. Heron was the first private company to raise a loan on the stock market back in 1965, and was the first of its kind to tap the European loan market. And despite his horror of exposing his master company to the demands of a share quote, he has been considering the idea of floating on to the stock market shares in some of his subsidiaries. This would have to be done on the basis of maintaining control in his hands, while leaving room to give executives in those offshoots extra incentives.

Ronson's way with his staff has been to display an attitude to them which owes more than a little to the example of his father, who was chairman of the group until 1974.

'If I die tomorrow, which God forbid, the company will continue without me. It won't grow as fast, without me to kick people up the behind and bully and cajole them. Instead of growing at 25 per cent a year, it would grow at fifteen per cent, that's all. But it would still be all right, and why should they do more? They'll still be doing well. Bullying and cajoling? It's talking to them like I'm talking to you now, telling them they should be doing this or asking why aren't they doing that, making sure everything's up to the mark.'

There are fifty key executives who run the business. As far as Ronson is concerned they are the ones who make the business tick, and he admits he could not do it without them. 'The biggest asset in my business is the loyalty and devotion of my employees. You can't put a price on that. The secret of working hard is to surround yourself with other hard workers. I want to employ managers who'd rather spend twelve hours at the office than twelve hours at home. And people like working for Heron because they know there's one man they can always go to for help or advice. I lead from the front. I don't work a nine-to-five day and expect them to climb Everest. When they're climbing Everest, I can tell you I'm well ahead of them up near the summit.'

But he recognises that loyalty has to work both ways if a chief executive is to expect that degree of devotion. 'I have to be loyal to them in return,' he said. 'That's why I don't sell businesses. When things are going badly in a company, the market's bad and there's nothing they can do about it, the last thing they want is the fear that I might sell the business. If I did that to one business, it would affect all the others.'

What about the executive who proves to be not up to the job? 'If he's a long-serving employee, then I would find him something else to do. If he's not a long-serving employee, then that's just one of those things and he has to go,' Ronson explained. Long-serving in Heron's book means three years or more.

But that family spirit has been diluted of late by the sheer growth of Heron, which has inevitably led to the influx of a stream of newcomers whose loyalty will take time to nurture. For them, incentives may cut more ice than the bullying and cajoling. 'Because of the growth of the group, we've taken on a lot of outsiders. Otherwise we try and promote from within. We're recruiting graduates now, though I prefer ones who have been out of university for a couple of years, so they don't think they know all the answers,' said Ronson. 'If we end up as a company run by accountants and lawyers, Heron won't be the business it is today, because we'll have closed our ranks to the kind of people I've employed.' Heron's head office houses 23 accountants already. But there is only one graduate on the Heron Corporation board.

Ronson has said many times that he sees himself as a hands-on entrepreneur. Although he can no longer physically visit every part of the group every week, he makes up for that with daily, weekly and monthly reports from each subsidiary, backed up by weekly management committee meetings and monthly brainstorming sessions so that he can look into each of his executives' eyes on a regular basis. They are not allowed to forget him.

Ronson said: 'My greatest personal strength is a flair for making decisions. I don't agonise over them. I don't have to sleep on them. I make them instantly. Not all of them, of course, are good decisions. But if 51 per cent are good, I'm on the right side. Mind you, I never make the sort of decisions that could make or break the company. If you study Heron you'll see that we are a very conservative business indeed. We don't go in for risk-taking.'

This attitude is all of a piece with Ronson's overriding desire to keep and maintain his hard-earned credibility. It is not stretching the point too far to argue that he has had to do more to prove himself in some corners of the City simply because he has not gone out of his way to ingratiate himself with the Establishment. That he has decided to go public, at least in the informal sense, says much for his long-term ambitions.

Now Heron is at a size where the financial community see the possibility of large fees coming to whoever can suggest a scheme which is to Ronson's liking. The loans he has raised have been worth several hundred thousand pounds to the bankers, lawyers and accountants who ushered them through. Ronson, in turn, has become aware of the need polish his image and explain himself, both in interviews with the press and across the City lunch tables.

What's it all for? He has said he wants to make a big acquisition in this country, worth maybe twice as much as the UDS bid. One reason is that, as with nearly all his deals, he thinks he could make a lot more money out of it than the present owners can. But it goes beyond that. 'I want to build Heron into a strong and lasting institution', he explained. 'It's just outside the top 100 companies in this country at the moment. It'll never be top, because you've got firms like BP and Shell up there. But I want to get Heron into the top ten.'

To pull off the sort of deals he would need to lever Heron into that sort of position, Ronson must have the acquiesence, if not the outright support, of the money men. He made his bid for UDS with some big pension funds standing alongside him. But Heron has doubled in size since then, and Ronson expects to keep doubling every few years for a while yet, without allowing for the effect of takeovers.

He summed up: 'It's a simple business. You just keep on going, straight on, day after day, putting in the hours. Perseverance. That's what makes the difference. We're not doing fancy share deals. It's just solid performance, year after year, and that's how you get credibility. The moment you miss a profit forecast, and for us that means a fall back in profits one year, that credibility goes.' Ronson's insurance policy against that possibility has been to be conservative about stated assets and profits, keeping something back in reserve in case he should need to deploy it in a bad year.

Yet Ronson shows few signs of wanting to amass a personal fortune. His salary ensures that he and his family are more than comfortable, and he indulges his fondness for cars with a handsome Bentley. But he has deliberately divorced himself from any direct interest in Heron, diverting most of the eventual benefits to charities aimed at helping the disadvantaged, 'whether because of environmental, social or physical handicap'. He is a tireless worker for the National Society for the Prevention of Cruelty to Children, which brings him in contact with other businessmen of a like mind.

When he is pressed to explain away his workaholic lifestyle, Ronson tends to claim that Heron is his hobby. But he does relax occasionally. He belongs to the Marylebone Rifle and Pistol Club, and sometimes hires a yacht from Heron Marine, one of the group's subsidiaries. The 1984 model, named *My Gail II* after Ronson's wife, had four staterooms and cost £2 million to build. It was sold to the Sultan of Brunei at a considerable profit. He also pays the company for the use of a British Aerospace executive jet.

But the impression Ronson gives is that these are no more than the trinkets of success. His true source of pride lies in his family life. He and Gail – a former model – have four daughters, Dera, Hayley, Amanda and Lisa. The measure of their importance is not only that he is patently intensely proud of them; he is equally devoted to shielding them from the arc lights of publicity – which he is reluctantly having to face as Heron's power and influence in its chosen fields becomes more apparent to the outside world.

Sir Clive Sinclair

Sir Clive Sinclair has expanded the lives of millions of people through the sheer force of his determination that we should share his vision of the future. His bespectacled, bearded face has become synonymous with the home computer boom to his legion of admiring disciples. Yet he is a shy man who finds it difficult to talk about his life, as if it were something that has happened apart from himself. Indeed, he appears genuinely uninterested in the past. That is done and finished with, and in any case cannot be altered; the future is what excites him.

Sir Clive's achievements speak for him to the extent that he hardly needs to speak for himself at all. His career has been a triumph of logical thought over the inhibiting effect of possible failure. In 1985 he appeared to be coming nearer to the brink of disaster than ever before. The previous year's launch of the QL computer had not gone well, and his controversial car/tricycle, the C5, was hitting a succession of snags. By midsummer Sinclair Research needed a fresh cash injection, which was offered by Robert Maxwell in return for a controlling interest. Barely two months later, Sinclair had recovered sufficiently to reject Maxwell's rescue bid. But in 1986 he finally succumbed to a takeover by Alan Sugar's Amstrad.

Clive Sinclair grew up with the idea that he would probably end up running his own business. His father designed machine tools and set the example for his own career. As Sir Clive sat on the chintz sofa in his small, neat, top-floor office above a corner shop in Knightsbridge, he recounted the early days: 'I loved being in my father's office,' he said. 'I wanted to start my own business, perhaps because he had had one and I liked the idea, I don't really know why. Another reason was that what I am is an inventor, and for me that is a question of getting ideas to the public. You have to have a vehicle to get your ideas across, because no one else is going to have the same commitment to them.'

Sinclair's childhood appears to have been reasonably well provided for, if somewhat nomadic. After attending a preparatory school near Guildford he went to three more schools, including Highgate in north London and St George's, Weybridge. None made much of an impression on him, and he left at the age of seventeen.

He was clearly intelligent enough to go to university had he so chosen. But he knew much earlier than most people exactly what he wanted to do. He was already reading original research papers, and it would have been an unlikely coincidence if any university had just happened to be doing a course which fitted his requirements. 'I was very bored at school,' he remembered. 'I preferred to learn by myself. I wanted to study what I wanted to study. I had reached the point where I wanted to follow my own path. I got out of the educational system as early as I could.' It has to be added that he has since become aware of a genuine debt to the educational system. After all, it does supply him with a steady flow of the raw material he needs for his business activities: trained brains.

At the age of seventeen, however, Sinclair's first problem was to find out how to start a business. He was not rash enough to think he already had the formula for success. His plans at this stage were taking on only the vaguest shape. He had not settled on what to make and sell, for a start. His father was not prepared to sink any more money into Clive's education by giving him the capital to form a company.

Instead, he hit on the smart idea of becoming a technical journalist. It was a much more open field than it is today. There were nowhere near as many titles, and there were even fewer recruits ready and able to write for them. As far as Sinclair was concerned, it was only a step or two away from having the freedom to do university research, without the unnecessary academic trappings and probably with more money into the bargain. Above all, it gave him the passport to look into any electronics business that took his fancy as a possible model for his own, as yet unborn.

He worked for *Practical Wireless*, and wrote small handbooks for the hobbyist. 'I learned far more than anyone who ever read the things,' he claimed. After three years he spotted what he hoped would be the platform for a Sinclair company launch: the pocket radio. This was in 1960, when such things were only just being introduced in the US and Japan, but could not be obtained in Britain because of import restrictions. However, it was not as simple as that.

'I just started a business as early as I could,' he said. 'Someone agreed to back the idea I had for making small radios, but they got cold feet, not unreasonably. I kept myself for about nine months with a bit of freelance journalism work. Then I began to run out of money and had to work again in a regular job.'

But the one vital quality Sinclair had while he was casting around was confidence in his own ability. He never imagined otherwise than that one day he would be running his own business, and that it would be a substantial business at that. A quarter of a century after he took the plunge, Sir Clive said: 'What holds people back from starting businesses is that they think it's very difficult. But it's not at all difficult. That is why I think the more people who start their own businesses, the better. It might well start a trend, and people won't think it's so magical to start a business. The rewards are very great, and the risks are not as big as people think. After all, at the start you don't have very much to lose, and yet there is no limit to how far you can grow. You have got to have something fresh to offer, but the one thing you have got to have is confidence.'

Like thousands of other small businessmen, Sinclair had to rethink his ideas and begin again in a more modest way. The second time around he was more cautious, beginning in his spare time and keeping his daytime job until there was enough work in the business to earn a living. 'I was living then at St George's Square, Pimlico,' he explained. 'I had this little room that served as my bedsit and workshop combined. My landlord said I had to stop running a business there, but he rented me a room round the corner that I could work from.'

At that stage he was offering his customers a very basic service. He took substandard transistors from the manufacturers, tested their actual performance and sold them to the hobbyist market on that basis. There was a built-in profit margin, because the transistors were otherwise useless to the manufacturers and the do-it-yourself electronics fans who bought them were able to get something that was good enough for their purposes at a lower price.

But it was never going to make Sinclair's fortune on its own, so he made the transistors part of an amplifier kit. This operation needed more space, so he rented a floor of a friend's premises in Islington. The amplifier kits developed into radio kits, and in 1962 he began to sell them under the name of Sinclair Radionics. Even though he had been in business for only two years by then, Sinclair had laid down two principles upon which he has based his business ever since.

The first was not to borrow. All Sir Clive's early expansion, from the day he began measuring transistors, has been financed by past profits – although he naturally made use of trade credit. The second principle was to make extensive use of mail order, rather than trying to sell through shops. Sir Clive explained: 'I went into mail order out of necessity. I had a market that was well identified, and served by people who read these specialist magazines. Everybody was taking tiny ads. Even if they had a lot of products, they would take a lot of tiny ads. Some took a page of them. I decided to take a half-page for just one product. It worked a treat, and people thought I was running a much bigger business than I was. I designed the product, a radio kit, ordered the parts, and placed the ad so that by the time I had to pay for the parts, I had enough orders from the advert to pay the suppliers. Companies were quite willing to deal with me on that basis. I rang the sales manager and asked if they would give me credit. To my surprise they agreed, but of course I didn't realise at the time that they effectively had to do that to generate their own sales. Anyway, I paid on time. We didn't borrow in the early years. It wasn't really caution; if I had had money, I would not have been able to make the business grow any faster. I felt uncomfortable with borrowings. I still prefer not to borrow.'

Over the years Sir Clive has elevated the initial necessity for mail order into an elegant theory of marketing hi-tech products which the shopping public may not understand and which the retailer will not therefore want to take a chance on. He declared: 'Mail order is a very useful way of getting a product across to the public.

Take the first model of a completely new product, like the ZX80 computer. WH Smith would not stock it, and the public would not buy it. Quite reasonably, they wouldn't know what to do with it. Equally, people will not buy on mail order if the product is in the shops. Mail order is a very useful way to get the story across. Not that big a proportion do buy on mail order, but they do see the ads, and that helps to prepare them for buying when the item appears in the shops.'

By accident, it was the emphasis on mail order which took Sir Clive up to his present Cambridge base – a happy chance, for it gave his business an academic gloss which did no harm to credibility, either then or later. It was another friend, already in Cambridge, who agreed to handle the mail order side. Sinclair then moved his whole business and eventually his family up there.

Until then Sinclair Radionics had been run on very similar lines to thousands of other small technology-based businesses. But the arrival in Cambridge, and the realisation that he could successfully farm out the chore of hatching and dispatching the mail order work, led him to make a radical break with convention. Sir Clive explained: 'At that stage I did it all myself: design, advertising, production, ordering. The competition was not very good, so it did not look too bad. I did not know the extent of my own ignorance, which helped. I was only interested in innovating.' But while he was and has consistently been able to keep ahead of the competition, he gradually discovered the extent of his ignorance, and even lack of interest in areas other than innovating. As his time was best spent doing that, and that alone, he conceived the idea of subcontracting everything else.

'It has always been my principle not to make a manufacturing commitment, which gives hostages to fortune,' he said. 'We have no capital base, except where we need it for a particular product. We don't want to absorb our very limited management effort in the management of large numbers of people, where we perhaps lack skills that other people possess to a marked degree.'

But the inevitable side-effect of this policy has been to put Sinclair at the mercy of his subcontractors, and from time to time there have been teething troubles. When he launched the first acceptable pocket calculator in 1972, the makers were not sufficiently acquainted with the technology needed to keep the calculator's power needs low so that sufficiently small batteries could be used.

But, at the then astonishing price of £79 for a pocket calculator, the buying public was willing to forgive – as, by and large, it has been with most of the gadgets that have flowed from the Sinclair drawing board ever since. He went on to expand the range of calculators and bring the prices down to pocket-sized, before competition became too fierce and margins were slashed. Once that happens, there is little room for Sinclair's innovating flair to collect its pay-off. He has to move on.

Unfortunately, he moved on from calculators to a series of problems, brought on as much as anything by trying to expand in too many different directions at the same time. This was the phase which saw the digital Black Watch, the first attempt at a pocket television and new digital metering equipment.

All three encountered difficulties. The Black Watch in particular suffered from a scarcity of the new type of integrated circuit microchip which it depended upon. Sinclair Radionics slipped into the red and found itself in the hands of the Callaghan Government's National Enterprise Board. Although this new relationship seemed for some while to be the ideal solution, it ultimately precipitated a crisis for Sinclair.

Sir Clive recalled: 'Our main business at that time was still in calculators. We launched the Black Watch. That was having technical trouble. Electronic instruments were profitable, but the profits were too small to sustain the losses on the calculator business and the watch. We developed the flat-tube TV, on which the research costs of about £500,000 had been shared with the National Research Development Corporation. But the actual launch was still a considerable risk, so there were two ways forward. I could press on, or I could have dropped that project and got the company right back to a very small business. I didn't want to do that, so I thought I had better get in some additional finance. N. M. Rothschild, the City merchant bank, helped me because I had met Lord Rothschild up in Cambridge, and he was impressed with what we were doing. I made a list of possible backers, with the help of Rothschilds, and just worked through the list. GEC turned us down, so we went to the next on the list, which was the NEB.'

Lord Ryder was heading the NEB at that time. He was all for Sinclair's plans and enabled the television, complete with two-inch screen, to go on sale in January 1977. It sold so well that a second version came out towards the end of 1978 at £99.95, less than half the price of the original. Meanwhile, the calculator range blossomed and Sinclair became one of the world's biggest suppliers of digital instruments.

But Lord Ryder left the NEB during 1977 and under his successor, Sir Leslie Murphy, an intense debate took place behind the scenes over the future of Sinclair Radionics. Sir Clive admitted: 'They then took a totally different view of us and they did not think much of the TV business. They did not listen to me. I had a personal computer under development. They tried to sell the TV idea to the Japanese. It was a real muddle. It should not have happened that way.'

Eventually the new men at the NEB told Sinclair that he could not stay in consumer electronics in competition against the Japanese. 'That was ridiculous,' Sir Clive argued, 'because the Japanese would sooner or later start competing in the instrumentation market. So I said I would leave with the consumer side of the business, at no cost to the NEB, who kept Sinclair Radionics as an instrument business, and of course it turned out for them as I said it would. It was finally a good solution to the problem. It meant I had got all the risk, but luckily I persuaded my colleagues to come with me. Some of them, like Jim Westwood, had been with me from the start.'

The NEB waved goodbye to Sinclair in July 1979, not long before the NEB itself was to be drastically reshaped by the incoming Conservative Government. Sir Leslie Murphy little realised that within a matter of months Sinclair was to take the world by storm under his new Sinclair Research banner with a computer costing less than £100 – the ZX80. That, as every computer buff knows, was followed by the ZX81, the hugely successful Spectrum and the more sophisticated QL. By 1984 the profits of Sinclair Research were running at £14 million a year and Sir Clive had been awarded a knighthood.

Such a rapid reversal of ill fortune was the product of a single-minded sense of direction coupled with growing acceptance by millions of people who, just a few years previously, would never have dreamed of owning a computer in their homes. Many of them grumbled at the delays between ordering a Sinclair computer and the delivery, but as Sir Clive conceded, one of the inherent faults of selling through mail order is that the publicity burst meant that demand hits a peak long before production can do so. But as long as he keeps well ahead of the competition, then the strength of the products can be relied upon to overcome any shortfall in distribution.

The effect of the take-off in demand for the ZX80 and ZX81 was that Sinclair could very quickly get back the cost that had gone into researching and designing them. This gave him huge freedom to keep his prices below those of the opposition. The ZX81 was being sold successively for £80, £70, £60, £50 and £40, while the cost of producing each extra unit was down to £20 or less. It was a virtuous circle of success giving the firepower for further success, and this 'halo' was duly passed on the Spectrum.

As Nigel Searle, one of Sinclair's closest associates, pointed out, it is largely a matter of thinking positively about the problems. 'He's a very, very positive thinker,' said Searle. 'He would never give up. He would always assume that if you are doing the right thing the situation can be resolved. The way the company is run is closely analogous to how you run a religion. There is no room for doubt.'

After fifteen years of working for Sinclair, Searle was still undecided how far Sir Clive believes his own propaganda. He explained: 'I think there are two people in Clive. There is an alter ego saying we are going to win, and there is also one of his troops inside him taking the orders. He is saying to us, we are going to win, but I do not know if he just feels he has to say that, or if he really believes it.'

However, it seems that doubt is allowed full rein when an idea is at the discussion stage. 'We never take votes,' Searle disclosed, 'and I think in that sense we are rather Japanese in our style, in that we argue things out until everyone agrees. Clive will fly a kite and it's only after it has reached a certain threshold that he becomes committed to it. Ideas incubate for some time and he bounces them off other people. So by then he has a consensus. He doesn't get into a position where there are ferocious arguments because then one party or another would lose face. And someone might hope that the idea would fail, so that they would be proved right. Ideas get killed not because people are opposed but because everybody yawns when they are mentioned.'

But Searle agreed that in any company like Sinclair Research where one individual owned 83 per cent of the shares and was actively involved in running the company, to a large extent the other executives had to accept that that individual was ultimately the person who decided where the company was going. 'Obviously there is a sense in which Clive's opinions and views influence other people more than anyone else's opinions do,' Searle admitted.

If Sinclair has a weakness, it is a dislike of the minutiae of management. 'In the very early days he was managing the company on a daily basis and it was gradually driving him crazy. He used to have an explosive temper, because of frustration. He's very impatient, doesn't suffer fools gladly and he is a very, very determined person. He works in a very immediate mode. He tends to inject ideas into the company: as they come to him, he will start discussing them. He then leaves it to other people to figure out how these things are going to be done. Clive is extremely logical in technical terms, but not in terms of dealing with people. He inspires people to do things which they would be hard put to explain why they are doing them.'

As Sinclair put it: 'We do not have any trouble keeping bright people, but we do have trouble getting them. The right environment and location are important, and a good *esprit de corps*, reinforced by company parties, company journals, that sort of thing. We have no difficulty in attracting people who want to work for us. It's more of a problem sorting the wheat from the chaff. We spend a lot of time interviewing people. We have found we have to headhunt one or two key people for certain areas. We look for creativity, experience, solid ability. They are almost all recruited for a particular project.'

The cream of those highly trained brains has been poured into Metalab, Sinclair's research laboratory at Milton Hall, near Cambridge. Although the early publicity for Metalab gave the impression that the recruits would be free to chase their dreams, they have in fact been tied closely to specific company projects. The Sinclair approach to research is for one group of people to take it from the concept to the market place. That puts the accent on the business outcome from the start, and means that work has to be agreed in advance. Sir Clive then lets people get on with it.

That approach, and the policy of subcontracting as much work as possible, have meant that Sinclair's payroll is remarkably small. Early in 1985 he had 140 people in Sinclair Research, his main company. Of these, there were sixty each in the computers division and in Metalab. The rest were employed on the flat-screen television, wristwatch radio and other electronic gadgets. There were another 35 based at Coventry, working for Sinclair Vehicles, the separate company responsible for the C5. Aside from the research teams most of these people were involved in the orthodox areas of sales and marketing, finance and administration, and helping Sir Clive to formulate the future policy of the operations.

Sinclair's idiosyncratic leadership style faced two important tests in 1985. One was the electric car, supposed to transform in-town motoring, and the other was the cash shortage at Sinclair Research brought about by the sudden downturn in the home computer market.

The car, known as the C5, provided a fascinating glimpse of whether the Sinclair technique would stand up to selling a mass consumer product in a market which almost every member of the public would claim to know something about. Whereas they were dazzled by the first Sinclair calculators and computers, no matter how rudimentary they were, the car was greeted with scepticism because the public had a firm idea of what a car should look like. They had been conditioned over several decades to expect a car to have four wheels and a roof, and be festooned with an ever-increasing number of gadgets.

The C5 was quite the opposite. It was the first cousin to the ZX80 in terms of their position in their respective markets – and about as useful, for most practical purposes. It was an open-topped three-wheeler with no reverse gear. Its top speed was fifteen miles an hour, it needed pedals to go up hills, and its batteries needed topping up after nearly every journey. So basic was it that a child of fourteen could drive the car and it did not need to be insured. In fact, some people argued that it was not a car at all, but a tricycle.

It was not long before the newspaper cartoonists and television comedy shows latched on to the C5. It sold quite well at first, but the public were not convinced and demand soon dried up. Later in the year the C5 company went into receivership, but Sir Clive still nursed plans to bring out an improved model.

To raise the money for the car project, he had sold £13 million of shares – leaving him with £100 million – to a group of City institutions, who would eventually want the flexibility to trade those shares on the market and be able to put an undisputed value on them. Originally, Sir Clive had wanted them to invest in the C5 because, reasonably enough, it was that rather than the computer business which needed the cash.

But although there would have been no shortage of backers for a brand new Sinclair venture, he was not willing to let them have the amount of information they were used to having so that they could make what they saw as an informed judgment. At that stage, the inside secrets on the car were too valuable to Sir Clive for him to let them go, however discreet the audience. 'You have got to keep quiet about new ideas and then come out in decent volume,' he declared.

So any outsiders coming in on the car venture would have had to invest out of blind faith or not at all. They evidently would not do that, so the alternative was to sell shares in Sinclair Research, where there was no lack of would-be backers and it was possible to point to a history of known success for them to go on.

Although Sir Clive insisted that the change in the company's status would make no difference to the way Sinclair Research was run, it often has the long-run effect of making innovative companies slightly less adventurous. The City soon makes the company aware of the need for steady profits and dividend performances, and that tends to make the directors play slightly more safe than they did before. A taste of that was provided by reports of a slump in home computer sales at Christmas 1984, which made the stock market so nervous that Sir Clive had to withdraw his own flotation.

Then it became clear that the drop in sales had left the shops with store-rooms full of unsold computers during early 1985. This meant that they were in no hurry to order new supplies, and from that moment it was inevitable that the share flotation was at least going to have to be delayed. Some of the City fund managers decided not to wait: they sold their shares privately, and the unofficial price slumped. 'Everyone who wants a home computer has now got one,' a disillusioned investor moaned.

When Sir Clive's bankers passed the hat round for more money, there were few takers. A deal was hurriedly put together whereby Robert Maxwell would acquire control of Sinclair Research. Maxwell planned to take a tighter grip on the firm's relations with its suppliers, and at the same time find new markets for the products, but Maxwell pulled out because, he said, there was no way of knowing how much money would ultimately have to be pumped into the business. In the autumn Sinclair instead signed a contract with Dixons, the electrical shops chain, to take a bulk order of home computer stocks. Less clear was whether Sinclair would still be able to come up with new developments with his old flair.

This put growing pressure on Metalab to come up with new goodies to dazzle the public. A major project was to develop the so-called fifth generation computers, the intelligent machines which could ultimately become more intelligent than man. In 1984 Sir Clive told the US Congressional Clearinghouse on the Future: 'I think it certain that in decades, not centuries, machines of silicon will arise first to rival and then surpass their human progenitors. Once they surpass us they will be capable of their own design. In a real sense they will be reproductive. Silicon will have ended carbon's long monopoly. And ours, too, I suppose, for we will no longer be able to deem ourselves the finest intelligence in the known universe. In principle it could be stopped; there will be those that try, but it will happen nonetheless. The lid of Pandora's Box is starting to open.'

That is Clive Sinclair the visionary talking, the chairman of Mensa and a man who now lectures the professors at Imperial College, London, whom he eschewed when he left school. He foresees a world where technology in its widest sense will liberate us from many of today's constraints, and he sees it as his mission to bring about that liberation. He already lives his own life as far as possible on that basis, aided by the considerable fortune he has amassed. He had his London house gutted to make way for a lift, swimming pool and roof garden. And – a far cry from the humble C5 – he has a weakness for the liberating effect of high-powered sports cars. He is also a lavish entertainer, throwing magnificent parties in the grounds of his Cambridge mansion.

Sinclair's great genius lies in his desire and ability to popularise the most complicated notions, and make them palatable to a wide audience. In his eagerness to show us his latest discovery, the first few batches are sometimes underpriced and prone to hitches. But the pace of invention is growing faster and faster, and Sir Clive is acutely aware of the competition breathing down his neck. As he put it: 'Technical excellence is the key thing. It is a very hard business to maintain. We have got to keep coming up with new ideas. I do not fear that we shall fail to do so; we have plenty more in the pipeline. What you must not do is show the Japanese the market and let them tool up for it before you are in there yourself.'

The alliance of Sir Clive's marketing tactics with his superb inventiveness are the key to the Sinclair dream. But what his career to date has shown is that he is able to bounce back from every reverse. Few people could copy him, because few have his technical genius. What he does provide is a blueprint for the ideas factories of the future, carrying as little baggage as possible and staying extremely flexible.

David Thompson

David Thompson is the sort of man you could miss in a crowd of three people, and he prefers it that way. 'I don't do anything,' he said, 'I only try to help the business and help people to achieve their ambitions.' But this unassuming and diffident entrepreneur, with the ruddy complexion and open manner of his Suffolk farming background, has a personal stake worth about £150 million in his master company, Hillsdown Holdings. Freed from any personal worries about money, he has been able to concentrate on developing Hillsdown, which was formed in 1975 to bring together his already rapidly expanding interest. It is a remarkable story of how enormous success can be achieved by keeping things simple.

Until it went public in January 1985, few had heard of Hillsdown. Yet it is the holding company for some of the best-known names in the British food industry, as well as the country's largest contract stationery business, and has interests in property, furniture and travel. The food brands include Lockwoods and Smedley's canned and frozen fruit and vegetables, Harris bacon, Daylay eggs – Britain's biggest egg producer – and Buxted and Harvest poultry.

However, as far as Thompson is concerned, the group is on the verge of even greater things. Although Hillsdown is seen primarily as a food group, he wants to spread its wings much further afield. 'We would go into almost anything,' he explained. 'It's really a question of having the right person to run a particular business. The people come before anything else. We do, however, like to make things that are pleasing to the eye. We want to market the best products and be the best in whatever we do. We would not like to get involved in arms. But if *The Sunday Times*, say, came up for sale, we'd be interested.'

This urge to have a go at just about everything was inherited from Thompson's father, Bernard. The family had been in farming, but had moved on to the high street between the wars with a chain of butcher's shops. Bernard diversified into grocery and provisions, and sold the chain to Fitch Lovell in 1953. Then, when meat was due to come off rationing the following year, he went back into the meat trade with a company named after himself, B. Thompson, which wholesaled off stalls at Smithfield, selling beef, pork, lamb, offal and poultry to butchers and food processors.

But in between times, Bernard had tried a number of other ventures which had little or nothing to do with the price of topside. David recalled: 'My father was involved in all sorts of things. He was always keen to try something new. He started the London Rusk and Spice Company, which dealt in commodities. He had been manufacturing ball-point pens. And he owned garages and restaurants. During the war he handled a consignment of 10,000 tons of whalemeat, which was on ration. At one time he had a fish cannery at Mevagissey in Cornwall.'

There was enough money in the family to send David to Hailey-bury, one of the leading public schools. He had insisted on leaving when he was seventeen, despite the pleas of both his father and headmaster that he should go on to university. 'I have regretted that decision ever since,' he admitted. 'I can still remember the headmaster saying to me, "Thompson, you are making a big mistake." He was right, and I have not let my son follow my example.'

Immediately after National Service Thompson joined his father and brothers Colin and Peter in the family meat business. Together they developed it from pure wholesaling to the point where it was importing from all parts of the world, often boning and processing the meat before it went on the hooks at Smithfield. B. Thompson went public in 1966. But within three years David, the youngest of the three brothers, had quit to go it alone.

The reason behind this decision was a merger which went sour. The Thompsons had a joint venture to market chickens with a poultry firm called J. B. Eastwood. In 1968 Imperial Tobacco, the Embassy and Players cigarette giant, was keen to expand in the food business and tried to buy both the Thompson and Eastwood companies so that they could then put them together.

This seemed such a good idea that the two firms decided that they would merge themselves without Imperial's help. The Thompsons were given to understand that Mr Eastwood wanted to retire, leaving them free to run the combined business. But it did not quite work out like that. Said Thompson: 'After the deal we found he had changed his mind, and wanted to stay on to manage the company. We had been used to running our own show, so I decided to leave.' Eventually Imperial took over the merged business of B. Thompson and Eastwood.

In 1969 David Thompson struck out on his own with a mixture of other investments and minor ventures covering property, insurance, engineering and do-it-yourself. 'All my life, I have been an investor in companies,' he explained. 'In a way, I am a merchant banker. For years I had been buying chunks of shares in companies; I might meet the directors on a Saturday to go through the figures, but, unless there was a problem, my involvement remained at that level. A good example is Hunter Plywood, now part of Hunter plc, which I started in 1966 with a Mr Hunter. I owned seventy per cent of it, but I did not spend much of my time actually in the company. I helped to make the important decisions, but I left the management to get on with it.'

After six years of this, Thompson decided that he had to tidy his sprawling interests into a manageable entity. That was the origin of Hillsdown, which was named after his home, Hillsdown Court. From the outset he began to apply his distinctive 'hands off' management technique.

Sitting in the modest and ultra-functional boardroom of his brand new head office in Hampstead High Street, Thompson explained his philosophy like this: 'If you come to me and say you want to run a business, we would both put money in for share capital and Hillsdown would provide the backup – legal, banking, property, insurance, and even stationery and travel arrangements. It's marvellous for someone who wants to run his own business, as long as he is prepared to work and put the company first for a couple of years, until the money comes in. We both give a commitment. We provide the support, and advice when necessary, and you provide the ideas and hard work. You say what you want to earn to continue to live at your present standard, with possibly ten per cent of any profits over and above that at the end of the year. However, if you don't make enough profit then there will be no extra at the end of the year, and if you make a loss you will have to take less next year. What I ask for is work, effort and dedication. It's up to you how much money you put in. There is no minimum. If you feel the business would happen faster if you borrowed, then fine. If you prefer to put less in and go more slowly, then that's understood. Either way, if you are producing the figures I'm content. It is also important that you are happy, because I believe the business always benefits that way.'

Once the new enterprise has been worked out, Thompson and his close-knit team agree targets with the manager. 'Before the year starts you have the budgets and projections for the year,' he said. 'There is a monthly forecast for each business. We sit down with you and say "What do you think you can do? Can you really achieve this?" The world is divided into pessimists, optimists and realists. We all think we are realists, but I can soon tell which category someone belongs to. Some people always meet their forecasts, while others are always being too hopeful. Then we learn to adjust for each person accordingly. That's all right, so long as they are consistent and the underlying business is doing well.'

Thompson added: 'At the start of each month we go through the figures for the previous month, comparing them with the forecast. If you promised a turnover of X, and it turns out to be only Y, we will ask what went wrong. You may say that an order got delayed, but it will come in next month's figures. That will be acceptable, but if it doesn't appear the next month we'll want to know the reason why. I like things in writing. Once we've agreed on the reasons for the shortfall in the last month, I'd like you to put that in writing and also what you expect to do about it. Then if it still goes wrong, month after month, it will all be down there and it will be possible for you to come to terms with it and we can sort things out. It will be easier for you to admit that you've been doing something the wrong way, if that's the problem.'

The yardsticks of success in Thompson's book are almost frighteningly simple. Thompson receives daily bank balances and weekly trading figures for each offshoot. All the companies have computerised reporting systems. The head office monitors look for the cash position first, then debtors – the amount the businesses are owed. 'We are very interested indeed in the number of days our debtors take to pay us,' Thompson said. 'We like to be paid on the due date, usually thirty days after delivery – we get concerned if it's thirty-three days. We also keep an eye on stock levels, so that they don't get out of hand.' Thompson then tries to ensure that each company makes the 'right' profit margin for the type of business it is in. That means that they must not be too far out of line with the average margin for the particular industry.

The secret of such a straightforward system is that the questions are less important than the standard of answers which he will accept. Hillsdown's record suggests that that standard is very high indeed. Stocks and debtors have been gradually squeezed in relation to turnover, while profit margins in the two main longstanding businesses – food processing and contract stationery – have steadily expanded. In the process, several thousand employees have been shed, but as Thompson explained that has been the result of decisions taken by the managing directors of the companies concerned. 'I was not involved with the necessary redundancies,' he said.

The stationery firm, Cartwright Brice, is a good example of how Thompson likes to develop a busines. 'I invested in that in 1965,' he said, 'and now it's the leading contract stationery firm in the country. It took a long time to reach that position. Every business has to get to a position where it takes off, but you have to spend a long time building a base. You have to have tremendous buying power. There is a lot of expertise in it, and a lot of work and dedication is required.'

Thompson has used that buying power to enable Cartwright to offer an all-embracing service to its customers, called the single-invoice system. This in turn adds to Cartwright's buying power, giving it the ability to offer an even better service. He explained: 'We can supply you with all your stationery needs. We will sit down with you and go through all the stationery you are buying at present, and cut the range down as far as possible, consistent with what you, the customer, want. You may be buying twenty different types of ballpoint pen. We might cut that down to one or two types. You will probably have several different types of pad: we will work out with you the best size and design of pad for your needs. We try to reduce the number of items as far as possible. As a result of our buying power, we can buy pens for perhaps half the price you can. Our products come from a tremendous range of suppliers. We can save you warehouse space, and we guarantee delivery in 24 hours if required. Nowadays we do continuous stationery and disks for computers.'

Behind that trouble-free explanation of a patent success story clearly lies a tough and uncompromising approach to what is a highly competitive industry. Yet Thompson convincingly gives the impression of shying away from the hard decisions. He said: 'If people want another month or three months to do something, we say fine. We have been criticised for running companies for a few years on the basis of our managers' "promised land". We will give people enough rope to hang themselves – and a lot of others too, if need be! I could never be accused of being impatient with managers, although sometimes there are mitigating circumstances. You might be a year out in your assumptions about a market, but we would give you the benefit. Now, however, we have a duty to the company and the public shareholders, so it is not so easy to give as much time.'

But the record shows that Thompson, his joint chairman Harry Solomon, chief executive David Bulmer and finance director John Jackson, can exact ruthless discipline from their subsidiaries when the need arises. In 1980, after Hillsdown had been operating for five years and the existing businesses were bedding down, Thompson decided to use his new base to expand in a big way on to his old stamping ground, the food industry. The growing power of the supermarkets had made mincemeat of all but the most efficient food manufacturers. Raging inflation during the 1970s had sent the cost of raw materials like animal feed shooting up, and the trends towards fresh food and away from red meat had severely hurt canners and butchers.

Thompson had kept in touch with the trade in a minor way. He was importing and exporting meat and pâtés, and selling portion-cut meat to restaurants and hotels. But in 1981 he took on one of the biggest casualties of the canning squeeze when Hillsdown paid

£3.5 million for part of Lockwoods Foods, which had fallen into receivership and was losing money rapidly. The following year the group paid £39.2 million for the poultry, egg, animal feed and meat trading interests of Imperial Group – much of which contained the old Eastwood and Thompson businesses taken over after David left.

In 1983 Hillsdown found Smedley's, the canned and frozen fruit and vegetable firm, buried under the name of TKM Foods and bought it for a nominal £1. A few months later, Thompson rescued FMC, the old Fatstock Marketing Corporation, after the National Farmers' Union Development Trust had failed to raise the money to keep it going. Then more poultry power was acquired, with a controlling stake in Anglo European Food Group, again for a nominal £1. In 1984 Thompson added pies, sausages and sandwiches to the corporate menu by picking up Telfers from Unigate, for yet another solitary pound note. To give more of an edge to Hillsdown's processing skills, the group paid a rather more than nominal £1 million for Perimax, a company which sucks bones clean of anything edible.

Within the space of three years Hillsdown had become a major force in Britain's food trade, giving it the potential to negotiate with the supermarket chains on something more akin to an equal footing. But before it could turn that potential into commercial reality, the newly-acquired businesses had to undergo the Thompson treatment. This consisted of pruning the workforce and top layer of management, tying the surviving managers' salaries closely to identifiable profits which they could influence, and spending millions on research and new equipment. Said Thompson: 'They have very good brand names. They are sound companies with good products. The middle management have been solid – it's been a question of the directors and the upper tier of management. The companies have got so big that there have been too many of them at the top. Normally with big companies a tremendous amount of fat develops. When we buy a new business that has been under big-company management, it's like a breath of fresh air for them. They can't believe it, and that's very exciting. It's all about sorting the wheat from the chaff and inspiring the right people, whatever the business.'

At Lockwoods, Thompson preselected the wheat by buying only the company's operations in Lincolnshire and Tayside. The new management found that, with a share of the profits to concentrate their minds, they could do without eighty of the 120 administrative staff. 'A £3 million programme of spending on computer-controlled processing equipment meant that a quarter of the workforce could be shed over the next three years, while capacity was cut to match demand. Colin Lazenby, Lockwoods' managing director during this period, reported: 'We were no longer on the defensive. We got support and were encouraged to make positive decisions. There was a friendly approach from Hillsdown, as opposed to a master and servant situation.' Smedley's was losing money at the rate of £1 million a month when it joined the group, but in the next year Lockwoods and Smedley's together made more than £2 million.

The poultry and animal feed companies were an altogether tougher proposition. Imperial had insisted on selling the whole batch, lock, stock and barrel, the good and the bad. They were losing money fast, and swamping the market with far more chickens and eggs than it could swallow. Three chicken hatcheries, three poultry factories and 59 of the 400 poultry farms were closed. Again, more than a quarter of the workers were lost while output fell by 500,000 birds and four million eggs a week to a million birds and 21 million eggs.

But Thompson agreed to two key organisational changes in this group of operations. One was to bring the feed mills under the direct control of Buxted and Daylay, so that they were responsible for their own feed costs and could develop the correct feed for their respective needs. The other was to sell direct to supermarkets instead of going through wholesalers, and at the same time put more value into the chickens so as to boost profit margins: fewer cut-price frozen chickens, more fresh birds and more ready-prepared dishes like chicken Kiev and chicken curry. Keith Lillington, chairman of Daylay, duly echoed Mr Lazenby's sentiments. 'It was the first time that we were allowed to decide for ourselves what to do,' he said. Nonetheless, while the poultry side soon started making money again, the signs were that Thompson was still asking his deceptively simple questions and not getting quite the answers he wanted. In the early part of 1985 Buxted's head office, sales and distribution were reshaped to cut costs and 'improve effectiveness'.

Before they joined the Hillsdown fold, both FMC and Telfers were in a forlorn state. FMC, a public company, had been wrangled over by the farmers who supplied it and, through the NFU, controlled it. That put FMC in an impossible position. Its management had no incentive to keep the business up to the mark, for if they turned in bumper profits the farmers would complain that they were not getting the best prices for their beasts. If profits were poor, as had often been the case in the years prior to the Hillsdown takeover, then the farmers' complaint was that the company was not getting a good enough deal out of the high street butchers. As for Telfers, it had become something of an orphan. It had been part of J. Lyons, who had never satisfactorily been able to blend it with their traditional cakes and ice cream business. It was sold to Unigate, who were unable to fit it in with their mainstream dairy activities.

Thompson set about reviving the two sets of demoralised management, armed with his own lifelong experience of the meat trade. Out went FMC's lavish head office just by Hyde Park Corner in London and the regional accounting centre in Sheffield. Each of the 41 abbatoirs was turned into a profit centre and, as usual, the manager's salary in each case was tied to an agreed profit target. Every abbatoir was linked by computer to the central accounting centre in Wiltshire. Money was spent on equipment to extract the last ounce of usable material from each carcass. Telfers, which was selling mainly to the catering trade, has undergone the standard Hillsdown cost-cutting exercise and concentrated on inventing new products for the supermarkets.

The full benefits of all this reorganisation will take time to show through. But Hillsdown and its main rivals agree that food will be one of the growth areas for the rest of the century. New tastes will be developed to tempt palates expanded by years of foreign holidays and exposure to a bewildering array of exotic restaurants on the British high street. And new technology is enabling the food manufacturers to meet the public's wishes more precisely in a form that is more convenient and long-lasting. One of Lockwoods' early successes under its new proprietor has been the foil tray, which is capable of storing food for months in a container that many people find more attractive than the can. And Ross Breeders, one of the batch bought from Imperial, has refined genetic selection so that hens can be bred to lay either brown or white eggs. Another breed goes under the toe-curling brand name of Mini-mum PM3: it is a hen which is small, so requires less feed, yet it produces normal-sized chicks.

Thompson explained: 'We look ahead ten years. Ours are very cyclical industries, food in particular, but they are getting better. In food you can see what's going to happen. If you see a lot more pigs being bred, you know there's going to be an excess of pigs in a year or two's time and prices are going to be squeezed. We normally do the opposite of what everyone else is doing. If there is going to be a glut of pigs, that's the time to be cutting back, and if everyone is cutting back then it makes sense to expand, because prices are going to be higher. There is no doubt about the growing power of the supermarkets, but the manufacturers are getting fewer. If the multiples are too tough on the manufacturers, they could get so few that this would have the effect of putting prices up against the supermarkets. Some manufacturers stand up to the supermarkets, and have been known to let their products be taken off the shelves rather than accept a price cut. We do not dictate a particular policy for our businesses. The individual companies set their own guidelines for their working relationships with the multiples.'

For a company of its size, Hillsdown runs an unusually small head office – a policy which is entirely consistent with Thompson's criticism of other top-heavy organisations. There are only the foursome of Thompson, Solomon, Bulmer and Jackson on the board. In a directorate of that size, none can be non-executive. Except for the legal formalities, board meetings are more in the nature of a casual chat. Thompson said: 'We all come up with ideas and discuss the ones that everyone's happy pursuing. I've often been outnumbered, and I've just dropped the idea. I'm only one member of the board, after all. We have recently gone into ice cream, and I'm very enthusiastic about that. We have got a lot of exciting ideas – some take a long, long time to come to fruition.'

However, he does not always take his colleagues' veto as the final word. He has on occasion pressed on, with a written guarantee that Hillsdown would not lose as a result. 'Sometimes, if I have been convinced of something, I would do it on behalf of the company and stand any losses myself. In other words the company could only gain, and that would be written into the agreement right from the very beginning.'

Between them, Thompson and the rest of his board embarked on a vigorous takeover spree in 1985 and 1986, picking up companies capable of adding to Hillsdown's mainstream food businesses, such as abattoirs, canners and packers, pig processors and coldstores, but also branching out into new areas. The group bought Needlers, the confectionery firm, a couple of ice-cream companies, Walker & Homer and Christie-Tyler in the furniture trade, together with an electronics business and an LPG gas supplier. While all that was happening Thompson further streamlined FMC and expanded its product range.

Thompson explained: 'In regard to Hillsdown Holdings' strategic outlook, I would say that the company will continue to be very much like an investment bank. By developing barriers to entry, the company will be assured of a quality of earnings and a solid base from which to develop and grow.' That suggests a hidden steel in Thompson's approach to business, belying his outwardly easy-going attitude. It would be hard to imagine anyone achieving as much as he has without such a tempered streak to prompt and reprompt the question a hapless executive may wish to evade. He has certainly had his share of past disillusionment: apart from the trouble at Eastwood in 1969, Thompson was scarred by the property collapse of 1974. 'I lent a lot of money in property in the 1970s,' he recalled. 'I guaranteed a number of people. I had to save a lot of companies because, when the problems came, these people were not able to meet their commitments. When troubles come, people start deserting you. We have had our traumas.'

What he has evolved is a system of checks and balances which, as near as is humanly possible, is designed to define that commitment and identify as quickly as possible any signs that it might be wavering. But it also has the virtue of giving those who want it the greatest amount of individual freedom and responsibility, and it may conceivably have a universal application – for those entrepreneurs who can keep their hands off the levers with as much control as David Thompson can apparently muster. 'I do what I do because I enjoy it,' he said. 'I have always enjoyed taking decisions. I try and give people what they want. Nobody's right or wrong about the way to go about things. People do what they want. Who am I to say what is the right way?'

There is little time in Thompson's schedule for life outside Hillsdown. He is proud of his grown-up family of a son and two daughters. In 1975 he bought a stud farm at Newmarket, which his wife looks after. Thompson admitted to visiting it 'every so often', which seemed to amount to four or five times a year.

'Yes, I love my work,' he conceded with a shy smile, 'and I often work six or seven days a week if that's what the business needs. I generally get in before eight in the morning. I might leave at six, or it might be eight, or sometimes midnight or beyond if we have a takeover on. The harder I work, the more I enjoy it – don't *you* find that?'

Mark Weinberg

Mark Weinberg is a man who is always on the move. Born in Durban, South Africa, in 1931, he moved to Britain at the age of thirty and has since swum restlessly through the shifting tides of the life insurance and pensions industry, taking in banking and unit trusts along the way. In the process he has created two substantial businesses, Abbey Life and Hambro Life, and made himself a multi-millionaire.

In 1984 Hambro Life was forced to call off an ambitious merger with Jacob Rothschild's merchant banking group, but by the end of that year Weinberg's business had been taken over by BAT industries, the tobacco giant, and was renamed Allied Dunbar. A relentless talker, writer and debater, Weinberg has always had the ability to recover from setbacks, however devastating.

He was widowed with three children, but in 1980 married Anouska Hempel, the Australian-born actress and proprietor of Blakes, the South Kensington hotel that the stars stay at when they are in town. Her first husband had been killed in a car crash, leaving her with two children.

Weinberg's father was a life insurance agent in South Africa for Sun Life of Canada, becoming in 1929 the company's top salesman in the world. In 1933, when Weinberg was two years old, his father died in an air crash. 'My memories of him are therefore in the form of received wisdom from my family,' said Weinberg, 'but it is a little more than coincidence that I am also in insurance. My family told me that my father would have liked me to be a lawyer. So I went to the bar in South Africa with no expectation at all of being in insurance. But the fact that my father had been in it predisposed me to the business.'

Weinberg's career has been based on the application of his

forensic skills to insurance, supplemented by an additional degree in commerce and a considerable personal flair for marketing.

Rising tension in South Africa during the 1950s made him conscious that his law degree was not transportable. The legal system there is different from anywhere else in the world, so if he wanted the option to emigrate he would have to obtain a degree elsewhere. He went to the London School of Economics at the age of 26 and took a British law degree to give him the flexibility he needed. There, he studied under Professors Jim Gower and Ash Wheatcroft, two men who were to have considerable influence at different stages of his later life. Professor Wheatcroft, a foremost tax expert, advised Weinberg in his early business career, lending credibility to some of his more controversial schemes. And in 1983 Professor Gower prepared a report for the Government on the wider question of investor protection, which naturally includes the life insurance industry.

Weinberg's first taste of London also made him aware of the contrast between the then rather staid UK life insurance industry and the more aggressive methods used in South Africa, which were based on the sales-driven insurance business of North America.

It was on his return home that his predisposition to insurance led Weinberg to begin doing legal work for Liberty Life Association, then a new locally-based insurance company. 'The first thing I did was to draft the rules for a new type of annuity for the self-employed, following a change in the law there,' he recalled. 'I saw the sales literature and thought that people would not understand it. So I found myself writing sales literature.' Today he still writes the brochures, because he has never found anyone better to do the job.

The Sharpeville massacre of 1961 made Weinberg decide to leave South Africa for good. And if he was going to go, he realised that he would be better doing so while he was still single. Donald Gordon, the chairman of Liberty, was so impressed with him that he asked if he would be interested in opening a branch of the company in London. Weinberg reasoned that the Sharpeville incident ruled that out as a practical proposition for some time to come. He wanted to make London his new home, but he felt that the London bar would be too difficult for him to break into.

'In short I needed a job,' Weinberg said. 'It was as simple as that. So I decided to go into business, and insurance was the one business I knew a little about. I did not have any thoughts of building up a significant amount of capital as a result. I had had a legal background, and barristers do not think of building up capital. They receive an income for life, for as long as they are able to practise. But the legal background, my degree in commerce and the Liberty Life connection taught me the mechanics of starting up. There is a lot of tax and law in insurance.'

Weinberg had no money of his own and he needed £50,000, the minimum amount of capital then required by law to start an insurance company. Donald Gordon put up a quarter from Liberty's coffers, and a similar sum came from another firm Weinberg was put in touch with, General Reinsurance of the Netherlands. The remaining £25,000 came from other ex-South Africans living in London, and his first office was shared with a South African accountancy firm. Weinberg had an option on a block of shares, which would give him ten per cent of the total when the option was exercised. In effect, his only capital at that stage was himself.

The six months Weinberg had spent in Gordon's office in South Africa made him realise just how archaic, in his view, the UK life insurance business had become. The range of policies had not changed in years. The people running the industry deliberately resisted change, believing that it would shake the public's confidence in them. The selling of insurance in Britain was similarly low-key, with the result that this country was one of the most under-insured in the world.

But the marketing side of Gordon's business in South Africa had fascinated Weinberg. 'It taught me how to simplify the product and the approach to marketing,' he said. 'In most companies that is done by different departments, and then it has to be gone over by the actuarial and legal departments. A new product can be buffeting around for a year before it hits the streets. The more you can pull these functions together, the less bureaucracy you get.'

So he set out to develop a company and a set of life insurance products which would be sufficiently respectable to be acceptable to the British public, but which would at the same time have the flair found elsewhere in the world. He avoided non-life business, such as house or motor insurance, because competition in Britain was fierce, and the insurer never knows exactly how much he might have to fork out in any given year.

Weinberg's first task was to gauge the opposition. He spent a week collecting brochures from the established insurance companies. More striking than the contents of those pamphlets, he noticed, was the fact that none of the people he visited tried to sell him a policy! The next and all-important decision was to pick a name for his company. This was a vital issue, because it would set the tone for the advertising and marketing effort.

'It had to be old and respectable, but unused,' Weinberg pointed out. 'I had several rejected by the Registrar of Business Names because they had been used back in the eighteenth century. Thames Life was one. The theory is that there might be some people holding policies with the old company, and a new one would cause confusion.' Eventually he tried a different approach. He returned to the pavement and walked around with five names to see how people reacted. Two were the names of existing and well-known insurance companies. But more people Weinberg spoke to said they recognised the name of Abbey Life as a respectable company they were sure they had heard of. In fact they never had. It was one of Weinberg's inventions, and it was the name he chose for his new company.

That was in 1962. For a year nothing much happened. Weinberg took on a couple of salesmen. He felt that selling was his weakest side, as he had never sold a policy himself, and still has not done so to this day. Instead, he bought all the books he could find and applied his lawyer's training to absorbing all the blackboard lessons he could from the pages of the textbooks.

Selling insurance policies, as with most other financial products, was and is strictly controlled by law. But within those confines, it was still possible to use the basic selling techniques of approaching the customer, rather than waiting for him to buy, and accentuating the benefits of life insurance – building a nestegg, providing for the family and, in those days, saving tax. 'If one of the salesmen came back and had done something wrong, we went over it from what the books said,' Weinberg recalled with a smile.

A big drawback of a new insurance firm, Weinberg discovered, was the would-be policyholder's constant question: why should I buy a policy from the one-year-old Abbey rather than one of the established names like the Prudential, the Royal, or Legal and General? 'It was difficult to give an answer,' Weinberg admitted. But instead of trying to ape the market leaders, he went for something new: insurance policies linked to the unit trust concept.

Instead of the traditional system of offering a sum assured, which might or might not be fattened by a complicated series of different types of bonuses – annual, triennial, reversionary, terminal – the value of these new policies was linked to the number of units a policyholder bought to go with them. He could follow the price of the units in the newspapers, in the same way as he would with a straightforward unit trust.

It was also a sideswipe at the unit trusts themselves, for by building in the life insurance element, the investment in the units attracted tax relief – a Government-blessed marketing weapon which lasted until the Chancellor of the Exchequer, Nigel Lawson, abolished the relief in his 1984 Budget.

As Weinberg is quick to point out, he was not the first to launch unit-linked policies. 'Never be a pioneer,' he advised. 'It's better to be second or third.' Previous attempts had been unable to pull completely away from the traditional types of policy, and still included such complications as the reversionary bonus. Not only did Abbey simplify all that excess baggage, but it also added in one totally new ingredient: sickness and accident benefit, paid for out of what would have been the traditional bonuses. In that way, Weinberg could claim to be offering tax relief on sickness benefit. It certainly brought Abbey to the public's attention, and gave the salesmen plenty to talk about on the doorsteps.

By 1964 Abbey was beginning to take off. The sales force had been expanded to eight, and Weinberg was working increasingly long hours to make up for the lack of bureaucracy. The blend of British and American techniques attracted several takeover approaches from US insurance groups keen to gain a foothold in the UK through a fast-growing company like Abbey.

Weinberg consistently turned them down because he wanted to build the business on his own, despite his consulting actuaries' pleas that the original £50,000 capital was fast being dwarfed by the growth of the business. An injection of fresh capital would have solved a lot of problems, but like many small businessmen before and since Weinberg was reluctant to let go. Then a personal crisis developed which changed his mind.

Weinberg's sister Myra had married a chartered accountant in South Africa, and the couple had gone to live in Israel. Weinberg's brother-in-law, a colourful character known as Smoky Simon, started selling life insurance, and like Weinberg he worked extremely hard. Weinberg takes up the story: 'In mid 1964 I got a telephone call from Myra to say that Smoky Simon had collapsed. His appendix had burst and he had carried on working, thinking he had nothing worse than a stomach ache. By carrying on like that he had aggravated it. I flew out to Israel. My brother-in-law was close to death for several days. He pulled through and is still alive today, but I decided then that life was more than working all day and coming near to death.'

When Weinberg returned to London he called his actuaries and told them he was willing to listen to the next offer that came in for Abbey. As it happened, they had had a call the previous day from Georgia International Life, who wanted to open a branch in London as part of a joint venture with ITT, the giant US conglomerate. They bought Abbey for £110,000. Weinberg made about £6,000 on his options.

He continued to run Abbey, and was soon joined by two old friends from South Africa, Syd Lipworth and Joel Joffe. Lipworth and Weinberg had been at school together. All three had studied law together. Lipworth had become a non-executive director of Liberty Life, while Joffe had defended several South Africans charged with political offences. Joffe, who had never worked in business before, went to Abbey and proved to be highly talented at administration. Lipworth has become the devil's advocate of the trio, putting every new proposal under a microscope of question and doubt before letting it through. The three complement one another, and their shared background has been important in helping them to reach a common attitude to the outside world. This has proved vital at critical points in their careers.

The principal effect of the Georgia/ITT takeover was to give

Weinberg the money to solve his problems on the sales side. He recruited Dan Dane as sales manager, who proceeded to build a sales force on traditional US lines, based on high pressure and high commissions.

Weinberg explained: 'The key thing is to have the absolutely best sales manager you can get and make sure he has a very good rapport with the person running the company. Every business depends on its own characteristics. Life assurance has always been a very difficult product to sell. People do not come to you. You have to go to them. And people do not want to think about death or old age. So even broaching the subject is not terribly easy. So you have got to motivate the salesmen so that they can accept lots of people saying no to them, which can be a difficult blow to take, time after time.'

The Abbey salesmen were motivated in two ways. Dane and Weinberg emphasised the importance of what they were doing, and gave them a strong financial incentive. Weinberg's style is very heavily influenced by American showmanship. When the top salesmen of 1984 were announced at the Wembley Conference Centre, the band of the Grenadier Guards played and 'prizes' were given. For the top salesman of the year there was a holiday, and a Rolls Royce was driven in to whisk him away!

Inevitably, this has led to criticism, both from the public and in the press, as some salesmen were bound to respond to the incentives too vigorously for some of those on the receiving end. The use of emotional blackmail to close a deal was one such accusation. Weinberg has always insisted that his businesses have attracted fewer complaints than the average for the life insurance industry, and that without some sort of financial encouragement it would be all too easy for the salesmen to stay behind their desks.

However, Weinberg acknowledged the problem by subsequently developing completely different techniques for reaching the public that did not involve putting a foot in their doorway. These primarily revolve round the notion of reaching preselected groups by post, offering life insurance as part of an all-round package of financial management. A variation on this theme was a link with House of Fraser, the department stores group, whereby the two companies would exchange mailing lists of customers and hold joint promotions.

A more immediate problem for Abbey in the late 1960s was the growing rift between its parents. ITT had formed the joint company with Georgia because it wanted to get into financial services. In this way ITT could match its money with the much smaller Georgia's know-how. But ITT, ever thorough, formed an in-house insurance department to monitor Georgia's contribution to the partnership, and before long discovered that in doing so it had hand-reared all the know-how it wanted. So ITT no longer needed Georgia, and it began trying to buy Georgia's interest in Abbey.

The trouble was that Abbey was growing fast by this stage. ITT would make an offer based on the latest set of Abbey's results, but Georgia would always object that Abbey had already moved on from that point and was really worth more. 'The history of those five years was a history of squabbles,' said Weinberg. 'ITT kept trying to buy Georgia, and in the end ITT got very tough. But as far as Abbey was concerned, it was like being hit by one parent in order to annoy the other.'

In 1970 ITT got its way. But the price was that Weinberg, Lipworth and Joffe left, along with Dane and other key executives. 'We told them that if ITT carried on the way it had been we would go, and we did,' said Weinberg. 'We pointed out that we would never be able to have complete confidence in them again, so it was better for us to go.' The episode demonstrates both the weakness and strength of Weinberg's position. In return for the quieter life he craved after his brother-in-law's brush with death, he had surrendered control and had had to build Abbey against a background of discord and uncertainty. But he had a trump card.

Life insurance is a service business, and the main asset of any such company is the skill and experience of its senior executives. Weinberg and his colleagues had that skill and experience, together with the confidence that if they had to they could start all over again from scratch. Weinberg was then 39, so he knew he had plenty of time left to recreate a substantial business.

He was also blessed with influential friends. Georgia had been advised in its negotiations with ITT by Hambros Bank, one of the City's most respected merchant banks. Hambros were impressed by Weinberg, and immediately offered to put up the money for a new life company. This time the name was no problem: Hambro Life Assurance.

Instead of the £50,000 he had had to start with eight years previously, this time Weinberg had £1 million from Hambros to work on. That enabled them to buy a small existing company, Sapphire Assurance, to save time and avoid some of the legal obstacles then being placed in the way of completely new insurance companies. The Hambro backing also gave them a precious five months to do nothing but plan before going into action. Weinberg himself had ten per cent of the shares in Hambro Life. That was to be worth £3 million when the company went public five years later. When it was taken over by BAT Industries in 1984, Weinberg's stake was worth £10 million – but that took no account of share sales during the intervening years.

As the financial journalist, Margaret Stone, records in a tenth anniversary tribute to the company, in the beginning Weinberg asked the executive directors of Hambro Life to set down the basic principles which each of them thought should govern the company from the start. Inevitably, it was Weinberg who took on the job of distilling their views into what were called four 'essential dogmas'. They were that the company should be profitable, free from conflict of interest, competitive, and should employ top-rate people.

While the first and last of these points are self-explanatory, the middle two were defined in less obvious fashion. Both were designed with the product in mind. Freedom from conflict of interest referred specifically to the areas between the company and its agents, or salesmen, between policyholders and shareholders, and between marketing and administration.

The products, or life policies, should be made equally valuable to the company and its agents by engineering the commission to that end. By unit-linking the policies, there should be no argument over the division of profits between policyholders and share-holders, because there would be no room for discretionary decisions. And the policies would have to be simple enough to appeal to both the marketeers and administrators. The policies should be made competitive by giving the investment managers the greatest amount of freedom.

What that five-month talking shop also laid down was the importance of having at the centre of the company a closely-bound group – known internally as the partners – who would meet frequently and informally as equals to thrash out the problems of the moment. This habit had developed naturally from the interplay between the original South African trio. But it was tactically the right approach for a business whose life blood is the new idea which has to be able to survive uninhibited criticism at the highest level.

Weinberg confirmed: 'That is very much the style of Allied Dunbar today. We have been able to avoid too steep a management pyramid. Instead of a plan going round from department to department, we can just sit down and sort things out. It's a teamwork-type company. I know there are companies where you have forty different subsidiaries that work independently with a few people at head office who pool the financial results at the end of the day. But we could not work like that. We are highly integrated.

'I am the conductor of the orchestra, if you like. Some people say that is not a very good way of running an organisation, but what you must do is to develop the people reporting to you, by bringing them on to a small number of broadly-based horizontal committees. We have eight people at working director level, then twenty more on the next level. So there are nearly thirty people within one level of one another. They each come from one strand of the business – legal, accountancy, marketing and so on – and you educate them in an environment where the partners are exposed to what's going on in other parts of the company. In that way they become educated in a broader sort of role.'

In such a centralised organisation, Weinberg's performance is paramount. And it has worked out that way over the past twenty years or so because he prefers it that way. He is happiest when he is involved in as many areas as possible. 'I am not sure whether I am a good delegator or a terrible delegator,' he said. 'It seems to me that I either delegate totally or I do not delegate at all.'

Sales is the one department which Weinberg can claim to have delegated totally. 'The moment I had confidence in Dan Dane or his successor, Mike Wilson, I left them to get on with it. I didn't even monitor what they were doing because that was and is their part of the business. But other things I kept far closer to. I am still more often than not significantly involved in the writing of the sales literature. I will chair a meeting and then write a memorandum on it, because I know the legal side and can save a lot of time that way. That makes it possible for me to get things done the way I want, but it takes up a lot of my time. I like the idea of the chairman with no paper on his desk, who just tells people to do this, that or the other and come back with the results, but I can't do it that way myself.' Indeed, the desk in his elegant office near Piccadilly, in the heart of London, is stacked with papers and files.

One reason for his avowedly hands-on approach is that Weinberg finds it difficult to get involved in a decision unless he has detailed knowledge of the issue. At the same time, by being at the top of the pyramid he feels he has an overview of the situation, so is best placed to make a decision quickly. That is why he believes that committees do not make decisions. 'In the meetings I run,' he said, 'I cannot think of more than two or three occasions when I have done anything approximately like taking a vote. If feelings are strong, people must express their views so that the person making the decision can make an educated decision, not a prejudiced one.'

It has to be said that such a distinctive approach works only to the extent that executives further down the line are willing to go along with it. Hambro Life took over Dunbar, a banking and fund management group, in 1982. But in the two years following, several of the Dunbar team moved on, some making little secret of their view that there was too much control from the centre.

In 1984 the group experienced its most serious reversal thus far, when it announced but later called off a merger with Charterhouse J. Rothschild, the then banking and industrial combine headed by Jacob Rothschild. The merger would have produced a complex financial conglomerate worth £1 billion, able to compete with the biggest of its kind in the world. It would have covered a wide range, from wholesale merchant banking at one end, to industrial investment and personal financial services at the other.

Although most comment at the time concentrated on alleged

conflicts between the two men, Weinberg disputed this. 'A company can only have one chief executive,' he said, 'but Jacob Rothschild was very happy that I should be that chief executive, and the board was entirely behind this. As a result, I do not believe that that would have been a source of trouble. The merger was called off purely and simply because, particularly in the market conditions that developed shortly after the proposal was announced, it did not hold water in stock market terms – and, particularly in a financial merger, you cannot fly in the face of the market. I happen to think that, if it had been possible to proceed, a great deal could have come out of the merger. But it did not proceed and there it is.'

Some months later, he reflected: 'CJR would have been interesting because there was no way that the two companies could have been closely integrated. That would have been a different challenge and I would have had to run the business in a hands-off way. It would have been interesting.' It does not sound as if it would have been a very comfortable experience.

But then, one of Weinberg's most useful qualities is his refusal to let setbacks get him down. In the first place, his approach is to minimise risk. 'I am very conscious of the downside,' he said, 'and I am always making lists of what can go wrong. But the most risky thing of all is being indecisive. Decisions will involve risks, of offending people or losing money. Some things will inevitably turn out wrongly, however careful you may be to avoid this happening. That is all right, as long as they are not what I call mortal risks, the sort that can bring down your whole business. If things go wrong, the important thing is not to let it get through to you, or worry you overmuch. I am reasonably robust about shrugging it off if things go wrong. I get the occasional newspaper article about me, and people say "That's a terrible thing they have said about you." I read it and that's it, let's get on. If you worry you will never take a risk or get anything done.'

But that does not mean that Weinberg finds it any easier than the rest of us to take the unpleasant decisions. 'Perhaps one of the biggest mistakes anyone can make is not to face up to shortcomings or failings amongst the senior management of a company brought about because the company grew beyond their capacity or they got caught by the "fat cat" syndrome,' he said. 'We have a very strong culture in Allied Dunbar, that the higher you get up the company, the harder you work. There have been numerous occasions where someone has, on the contrary, thought that he could sit back and do nothing, and I have allowed a delay of a year or two in making the decision that he has to go. The longer you leave it the more painful it is for both sides. It happens eventually, when it blows up in your face. It's much more agonising then.'

The whole bias of the life insurance business makes it vitally important to get the decisions right from the onset. A life company's different flows of cash from policy premiums and investment returns, offset by policy claims, redemptions and overheads, are too complicated to monitor on a day-to-day basis. But, because so much of it is based on written contracts, it is fairly predictable. 'We are very much concerned, when designing a product, to build in the profit. Secondly, we make sure that the system is monitoring expenses,' said Weinberg. 'These are the two ways you can go wrong in a life company.'

Two ways is not too many. Most businessmen could live with that. And Allied Dunbar minimises the risk further by running computer simulations to ensure that everything is moving in the right direction. It would be hard to do that in a general insurance company, handling such uncontrollable risks as motor, fire and theft.

However, Weinberg wants to widen the scope of Allied Dunbar without exposing it to much more risk. He explained: 'I feel very strongly that most people do not enjoy shopping around for financial services. They are conscious of the fact that they do not have the expertise to distinguish between the products offered by one institution or another, or even to decide which sort of institution to go to, to meet a particular problem or need. I believe that if an organisation they trust, acting through an individual with whom they have established a personal relationship, offers them a wide range of services and saves them from having to shop around, they will be extremely relieved. This is the route we are following.'

Of course, Weinberg is having to pursue this latest path within the constraints of being subject to a parent company once more. Not only that: Allied Dunbar's operations will have to chime in with those of BAT's other insurance subsidiary, Eagle Star. Only time will tell how well this arrangement will work, but the previous experience of Weinberg, Lipworth and Joffe under ITT suggests that there will be testing periods for both sides.

Weinberg, meanwhile, is steadily burnishing his image as the conscience of the British life insurance industry. In 1984 he served on the Governor of the Bank of England's committee to advise on how the City should be regulated. And in 1985 he was appointed chairman of the Marketing of Investments Board, the body which the Government was setting up to oversee insurance, pensions and unit trusts.

The MIB was eventually absorbed into the Securities and Investments Board, the Government's designated agency for enforcing the new Financial Services Act. Weinberg duly joined that board and continued his former role in the new guise.

Profiles

Sir Nigel Broackes

1934 Born
1950 Left Stowe
1956 First West End development, Green Park House
1958 Managing director of Eastern International Property
       Investments (later Trafalgar House)
1962 Deputy chairman of Trafalgar House
1963 Trafalgar House goes public
1964 Trafalgar House takes over Bridge Walker; Victor Matthews
       joins the group
1965 Corporation Tax introduced
1966 Eric Parker recruited from Taylor Woodrow
1967 Trafalgar House takes over Ideal Building Corporation
1968 Trafalgar House takes over Trollope & Colls
1969 Chairman of Trafalgar House
1969 Trafalgar House starts buying shares in Savoy Hotel
1971 Trafalgar House takes over Cunard Steamship Company
1976 Trafalgar House takes over Ritz Hotel
1977 Trafalgar House takes over Beaverbrook Newspapers
1978 Trafalgar House sells Savoy shares to Grand Metropolitan
1980 Chairman of London Docklands Development Corporation
1982 Fleet Holdings floated on stock market
1984 Resigns from LDDC
1984 Knighted
1984 Chairman of EuroRoute

Sir Terence Conran

1931 Born
1947 Left Bryanston; joined Central School of Art and Design
1951 Festival of Britain
1952 Opens Bethnal Green Workshop
1954 Begins Soup Kitchens
1956 Opens Orrery Restaurant, King's Road
1956 Starts Conran Design Group
1959 Starts Conran Contracts
1962 Starts furniture factory, Thetford
1964 Opens first Habitat shop
1966 Publishes first catalogue
1968 Merges with Ryman
1970 Ryman merger ends
1971 Opens Neal Street Restaurant
1973 Opens first overseas Habitat, Paris
1977 Habitat opens in New York
1979 Joins board of J. Hepworth
1981 Habitat goes public, merges with Mothercare
1981 Boilerhouse Project opens, Victoria & Albert Museum
1983 Knighted
1983 Habitat Mothercare buys Heals
1983 Resigns as chairman of J. Hepworth
1983 Habitat Mothercare buys Richard Shops
1983 NOW launched
1983 Butler's Wharf project begins
1985 Habitat Mothercare merges with British Home Stores to
     form Storehouse

Michael Golder

1944 Born
1966 Graduates from London School of Economics
1973 Buys Kennedy Brookes
1980 Kennedy Brookes takes over Alfresco Feasts: Roy
      Ackerman joins the group
1980 Kennedy Brookes shares begin to be traded on the 'over the
      counter' market
1981 Kennedy Brookes shares floated on the Unlisted Securities
      Market
1981 Kennedy Brookes takes over Mario and Franco Restaurants
1983 Kennedy Brookes takes over Wheeler's Restaurants
1983 Maxim's de Paris opens, Panton Street
1984 Laurence Isaacson becomes a director
1984 Kennedy Brookes buys The Ivy Restaurant
1984 Trocadero opens
1984 Kennedy Brookes takes over The London Pavilion
1984 Kennedy Brookes takes over Café des Amis
1985 First Wheeler's Restaurant franchises sold

Harry Goodman

1939 Born
1954 Left school
1966 Buys Sidcup Travel (later Sunair)
1971 Sells Sunair to Cunard; Goodman leaves after Cunard is
      taken over by Trafalgar House
1972 Goodman buys Intasun
1974 Clarksons ceases trading
1978 Air Europe formed
1980 First package holidays to Miami
1981 Intasun floated on the Unlisted Securities Market
1982 Laker Airways ceases trading
1983 Intasun takes over Club 18–30
1985 Intasun takes over Global Holidays
1985 Goodman changes the name of his holding company to
      International Leisure Group

James Gulliver

1932 Born
1960 Joins Urwick Orr
1965 Joins Fine Fare
1967 Chairman of Fine Fare, director of Associated British Foods
1973 Buys 29 per cent of Oriel Foods, goes on board
1974 Oriel taken over by RCA
1977 Leaves Oriel
1977 Becomes director of Alpine Holdings
1979 Buys 20 per cent of Louis C. Edwards (renamed Argyll
          Foods), becomes director
1979 Becomes director of Amalgamated Distilled Products
1979 Argyll takes over Yorkshire Biscuits
1979 Argyll takes over Furniss & Co.
1980 Argyll takes over Cordon Bleu
1980 Argyll takes over Dalgety Frozen Foods
1980 Argyll takes over Morgan Edwards
1980 Argyll takes over Freezer Fare
1981 Argyll takes over Oriel Foods
1982 Argyll takes over Pricerite
1982 Argyll takes over Allied Suppliers
1983 Argyll merges with Amalgamated Distilled Products
1983 Alpine Holdings taken over by Kean and Scott
1985 Argyll bids for Distillers

John Gunn

1942 Born
1962 Graduates from Nottingham University
1963 Joins Barclays Bank
1968 Joins Astley and Pearce
1975 Astley and Pearce taken over by Gerrard and National; Exco formed to hold executives' shares in Astley
1979 Gunn leads management buyout of Astley
1981 Exco buys into Telerate
1981 Exco goes public
1982 Exco buys 75 per cent of WICO, Far Eastern stockbroker
1982 Exco starts money broking in Japan
1983 Exco buys control of Telerate
1983 Exco buys 50.1 per cent of Gartmore Investment Management
1984 Exco buys 29.9 per cent of Galloway and Pearson, London stockbrokers
1984 Exco buys 76 per cent of Williams, Cooke, Lott and Kissack, to be an inter dealer broker in new government stocks market
1984 Exco buys 40 per cent of Blackman, Garlock Flynn & Co., US real estate broker
1985 Exco sells Telerate
1985 Gunn quits Exco
1985 Gunn joins British and Commonwealth Shipping

Noel Lister

1928 Born
1947 Joins Bowmans, Camden Town furniture store
1951 Starts own business as trader
1955 Meets Donald Searle, co-founder of MFI
1964 Mullard Furniture Industries founded
1967 First retail warehouse opened
1970 Donald Searle killed in gliding accident
1971 MFI Warehouses goes public
1977 Name changed to MFI Furniture Centres
1979 MFI Furniture Group formed, to separate retailing and
         property activities
1985 MFI merges with Associated Dairies

Stephen Marks

1946 Born
1963 Plays tennis at Junior Wimbledon
1963 Joins Sheraton, coat maker
1969 Starts designing under 'Stephen Marks' label
1972 'French Connection' label launched
1972 Makes first trip to India and Far East
1973 French Connection shop opens in Top Shop, Oxford Street
1976 'French Connection No. 2' menswear launched
1976 Signs licensing deal with Best of All Clothing in US
1978 Begins export to France
1983 Connections shop opens in New York
1983 French Connection Group shares floated on Unlisted
        Securities Market
1984 French Connection Group buys 50 per cent of Ronnies Slax
        N Shirtails, owner of Best of All Clothing
1985 First Nicole Farhi shop opens

Robert Maxwell

1923 Born
1939 Escapes from Czechoslovakia, joins British Army
1944 Awarded Military Cross
1945 Head of Foreign Office Press Section, Berlin
1948 Robert Maxwell & Co. founded
1949 Maxwell takes over Butterworth Springer
1951 Pergamon Press formed out of Butterworth Springer
1951 Maxwell takes over Simpkin Marshall
1955 Simpkin Marshall goes into liquidation
1964 Pergamon Press goes public
1964 Maxwell elected to Parliament
1968 Pergamon bids unsuccessfully for *News of the World*
1969 Merger with Leasco Data Processing announced and
      aborted; Maxwell voted off Pergamon board; shares
      suspended
1970 Maxwell defeated in General Election
1974 Maxwell regains control of Pergamon as private company
1975 Maxwell helps to launch *Scottish Daily News* as a workers'
      cooperative – closes after a few months
1981 Pergamon buys control of British Printing Corporation
1984 Pergamon buys Mirror Group Newspapers from Reed
      International
1984 Pergamon buys Rediffusion Cable

Gerald Ronson

1939 Born
1954 Leaves school to work for father
1956 Ronsons decide to quit furniture business, go into property
1958 Heron develops first block of flats, Heron Court, Lancaster Gate, London W.2.
1962 Ronson becomes millionaire in his own right
1965 Heron is first private company to raise a loan through the Stock Exchange
1965 Heron goes into housebuilding
1966 First Heron service station opened
1970 Heron buys Swain Group, owner of the Rolls-Royce distributors, H. R. Owen
1972 Heron buys Scottish Automobile; founds Heron Motor Group
1974 Succeeds father as chairman of Heron
1975 Heron buys Suzuki (Great Britain), motorcycle distributor
1977 Heron buys National Insurance and Guarantee Corporation
1978 Heron moves into US
1980 Heron takes over Pima Savings and Western American Mortgage of Arizona
1981 Heron bids for Associated Communications Corporation; outbid by Robert Holmes a'Court
1982 Heron buys 12,500 acres from Howard Hughes estate in Tucson
1982 Heron launches Lancar, distributor for Lancia cars
1983 Bids in a consortium for UDS Group – outbid by Hanson Trust
1983 Heron buys Videoform and Media Home Entertainment
1983 Heron issues 100 million Swiss Franc loan stock
1983 Heron buys Fidelity Federal Savings of Douglas, Arizona
1984 Heron buys Relay Video

Sir Clive Sinclair

1940 Born
1957 Leaves St. George's, Weybridge
1958 Joins Bernards Publishers
1962 Sinclair Radionics founded
1967 Sinclair Radionics moves to Cambridge
1972 Executive pocket calculator launched
1973 Cambridge range of pocket calculators launched
1974 Matchbox Radio launched
1975 Black Watch launched
1976 National Enterprise invests in Sinclair Radionics
1977 Microvision, the first pocket television, launched
1979 Sinclair leaves Sinclair Radionics, starts Sinclair Research
1980 ZX80 personal computer launched
1981 ZX81 personal computer launched
1982 Spectrum personal computer launched
1983 New flat-screen pocket TV launched
1983 Sinclair knighted
1984 QL personal computer launched
1985 C5 car launched
1985 Sinclair Vehicles in receivership
1986 Personal Computer business taken over by Amstrad

David Thompson

1936 Born
1953 Left Haileybury
1955 Joins B. Thompson, family meat business
1965 Thompson invests in Cartwright Brice
1968 B. Thompson merges with J. B. Eastwood
1969 Thompson leaves B. Thompson to run own business
1975 Hillsdown Holdings founded
1981 Hillsdown acquires part of Lockwoods Foods
1982 Hillsdown buys Buxted, Daylay, Nitrovit, Ross Breeders,
       Ross Poultry and meat trading interests of B. Thompson
       from Imperial Group
1982 Hillsdown buys A. J. Mills
1982 Hillsdown buys TKM Foods (Smedley's)
1983 Hillsdown buys FMC
1983 Hillsdown buys Anglo European Food Group
1984 Hillsdown buys Perimax
1984 Cartwright Brice buys contract stationery and printing
       equipment businesses from Inveresk Stationery
1985 Hillsdown goes public

Mark Weinberg

1931 Born
1962 Abbey Life founded
1964 Georgia International Life invests in Abbey
1965 Syd Lipworth and Joel Joffe join Abbey
1970 ITT takes over Abbey; Weinberg, Lipworth, Joffe and
        others leave
1971 Hambro Life Assurance founded
1972 Hambro Tax Guide published for the first time
1975 Prudential Insurance of US buys stake in Hambro Life
1976 Hambro Life goes public
1982 Hambro Life buys Dunbar
1984 Hambro Life proposes to merge with Charterhouse J.
        Rothschild, but plan falls through
1984 BAT Industries takes over Hambro Life
1985 Weinberg appointed chairman of Marketing of Investments
        Board and joins the Securities and Investments Board

Index